"Freedom. That is what I am beginning to grasp. Through the reading of *Exhale*, I found myself sensing new freedom in my life as I began to put into practice the principles Amy and Cheri lay out so clearly. I'm taking new steps toward losing who I'm not, loving who I am, and living my one life well thanks to this book! I'm so grateful for it!"

Lynn Cowell, Proverbs 31 speaker; author, *Make Your Move: Finding Unshakable Confidence Despite Your Fears and Failures*

"In a culture saturated with pressure to always do more and be more, Amy Carroll and Cheri Gregory offer a different way. Like fresh air to women who can't catch a breath, *Exhale* lifts the burdens you were never meant to bear and then infuses your day with compassion, wisdom, and practical steps to live your one life well. This book isn't one more to-do; it's permission to do less."

Michele Cushatt, author, *I Am: A 60-Day Journey to Knowing Who You Are Because of Who He Is*

"With hard-won wisdom, authenticity, and hearts for the truth of Scripture, Amy Carroll and Cheri Gregory deliver an approachable empowerment to spiritual and emotional growth. In these pages discover that you're not alone, change is possible, and hope can infuse your present and future life. A well-written, practical book."

Mary DeMuth, author, *We Too: How the Church Can Respond Redemptively to the Sexual Abuse Crisis*

"*Exhale* feels like a good friend who just walked through the door and invited you to rest. That friend knows how tired you are, how exhausted you are from trying to be all, do all. I love how gentle and funny and wise this book is, and I highly recommend it to any woman needing a deep, refreshing breath of clarity."

Suzanne Eller, international speaker; bestselling author; cohost, *More Than Small Talk* podcast

"Amy and Cheri are the wise friends who have been there and who will take y⟨...⟩, and share just what you need to hear to begin a journey of empowerment to finding your fullest life in Christ. You are created for less—less worry, less self-judging, and less second-guessing. You are also created for more—more joy, more happiness, and more fulfillment. *Exhale* is a beautiful guide, full of wisdom and grace, to a better you. I can't wait to read it again!"

Susy Flory, *New York Times* bestselling author; director, West Coast Christian Writers Conference

"Take a deep breath. You officially have permission to stop being 'Super Woman,' doing all the things, and instead bask in exactly who God has made you to be. In *Exhale*, Amy and Cheri have given us a precious gift. It's the gift of Bible stories showing us *what* pieces of ourselves we can ditch, practical advice on *how* to ditch them, and the beautiful hope that emerges in us *when* we allow God to transform us. You do not want to miss this book. Every page is like a breath of fresh air."

Maria Furlough, speaker; author, *Breaking the Fear Cycle* and *Confident Moms, Confident Daughters*

"Have you ever suddenly realized you're holding your breath? Your stomach is tight, your shoulders tense, your smile forced. Then, *whoosh*, you breathe and everything changes. This book is like that for a stressed-out woman's heart. You read and everything changes."

Holley Gerth, bestselling author, *You're Already Amazing*

"This book is the breath of fresh air we've all been longing and looking for. If you're feeling burned out or overwhelmed, *Exhale* will show you how to leave your frazzled ways behind to embrace a life of fulfillment and freedom."

Lauren Gaskill, founder and president, She Found Joy; author, *Into the Deep: Diving Into a Life of Courageous Faith*

"Amy and Cheri shine here. Their conversational style makes this a breeze to read, yet the impact is life-changing. How many women do you know who truly celebrate—and steward—how God made them? Want to become that woman? Then *Exhale* is a must-read."

Lisa T. Grimes, coauthor, *Remember Who You Are*;
managing director, Habergeon

"I know what it's like to be so exhausted from trying to meet everyone's expectations, so stressed by circumstances, and so beaten down by problems and people that simply breathing feels like a challenge. *Exhale* is a book I so could have benefited from during those trying seasons. Amy and Cheri's tips and encouragement help us all learn to breathe again as we discover how to rest in who we are and whose we are, so we can fully embrace and enjoy the life God has given us."

Tracie Miles, author and Proverbs 31 speaker;
director, COMPEL Training

"Maybe you long to lay down heavy burdens or embrace the future with hope and optimism. *Exhale* will serve as your friendly and practical guide. It's time to step out into the life you were meant to live."

Arlene Pellicane, speaker and podcaster;
author, *31 Days to Becoming a Happy Wife*

"Hey, you. The one gripping your list, making your plan. Worrying, stressing, and wondering how you'll ever please everyone and get it right. Aren't you tired of holding your breath? Aren't you ready to *exhale*? With humor, kindness, vulnerability, and joy, Amy and Cheri pack each chapter of this book with precious and powerful insights from God's Word, along with tender guidance on how we can exhale, move forward, and breathe."

Shannon Popkin, speaker and blogger; author, *Control Girl: Lessons on Surrendering Your Burden of Control from Seven Women in the Bible*

"Carroll and Gregory pour out hard-won wisdom like a balm for dependable women. Through candid stories, pivotal observations, and aha moments, *Exhale* delivers clarity and assurance. Breathe deeply of

God's love and walk confidently, with purpose, as you interact with this gold mine of goodness."

Katie M. Reid, Bible teacher; author, *Made Like Martha: Good News for the Woman Who Gets Things Done*

"Amy and Cheri are the friends I wish I had in my real life—the kind who love you enough not to leave you in the pit and who offer a hug as they help you navigate your way forward with practical tools, simple swaps, and honest encouragement."

Crystal Stine, speaker and blogger; author, *Holy Hustle: Embracing a Work-Hard, Rest-Well Life*

"Amy Carroll and Cheri Gregory use their personal experiences to expose the common potholes that trip too many of us on our journey to becoming and appreciating who we are. Their understanding and helpful guidance will add chuckles and insights to improve your trek and keep you on track."

Debbie W. Wilson, cofounder, Lighthouse Ministries; author, *Little Women, Big God*

"*Exhale* authors Cheri Gregory and Amy Carroll offer women a respite, giving them permission to take the packs off their backs, sit for a spell, and breathe deep with God. An excellent resource written by two gifted communicators."

Ginny L. Yttrup, author, *Words* and *Invisible*

exhale

exhale

LOSE WHO YOU'RE NOT,
LOVE WHO YOU ARE,
LIVE YOUR ONE LIFE WELL

AMY CARROLL AND
CHERI GREGORY

BETHANYHOUSE

a division of Baker Publishing Group
Minneapolis, Minnesota

© 2019 by Amy Carroll and Cheri Gregory

Published by Bethany House Publishers
11400 Hampshire Avenue South
Bloomington, Minnesota 55438
www.bethanyhouse.com

Bethany House Publishers is a division of
Baker Publishing Group, Grand Rapids, Michigan

Printed in the United States of America

Library of Congress Cataloging-in-Publication Data
Names: Carroll, Amy, author.
Title: Exhale : lose who you're not, love who you are, live your one life well / Amy
    Carroll, Cheri Gregory.
Description: Minneapolis : Bethany House, a division of Baker Publishing Group, 2019.
Identifiers: LCCN 2018053559 | ISBN 9780764232732 (trade paper : alk. paper) | ISBN
    9781493418770 (ebook)
Subjects: LCSH: Women—Religious aspects—Christianity. | Identity (Psychology)—
    Religious aspects—Christianity. | Christian women—Religious life.
Classification: LCC BT704 .C39 2019 | DDC 248.8/43—dc23
LC record available at https://lccn.loc.gov/2018053559

Cover design by Kathleen Lynch/Black Kat Design

Amy Carroll represented by The Blythe Daniel Agency

Cheri Gregory represented by The Steve Laube Agency

19 20 21 22 23 24 25   7 6 5 4 3 2 1

To Mom and Dad,
the first and most treasured
seed senders in my life
– Amy

To Daddy,
I'm so glad you picked me
to be your daughter.
– Cheri

Contents

Foreword

When was the moment?

The moment the world told you that you were not enough.

Or in my case, just way too much.

For me, it was in fourth grade, my first day at a new school. I was so grateful that my new teacher had assigned a "friend," Valerie, to show me how to maneuver all things elementary school. She sat next to me during class and told me which books to pull out, pointed out the pencil sharpener, and most importantly, showed me where the girls' bathroom was.

Then it was time for lunch. I grabbed my *Laverne & Shirley* lunch box and headed for the picnic tables. Valerie stopped me cold and said, "I don't think I have to have lunch with you. I think I get to have a break," and walked on to be with her real friends.

Not the friend that was assigned to her.

I sat alone that day on the hard wooden bench and vowed to do everything I could to not be the person everyone needed a break from.

And at times, it has worked. I've kept who I am hidden so that I don't put my needs on others. I've worked hard to make sure the world doesn't see the person I am trying so hard to keep pushed down. But let me tell you, that is an exhausting way to live.

So, my friend, when was the moment? The moment you found out you were too . . . (fill in the blank).

Because let's be clear—the world doesn't have the time or energy to figure you out. So it squeezes and compacts you until your only concern is that everyone around you is comfortable. You make yourself small so that everyone else is not inconvenienced, bothered, or put out by the too-muchness of you.

But why did we ever start to believe the lie that being who God designed us to be is something to be contained for the convenience of others?

And that is why this book, *Exhale*, is what I needed, when I needed it.

You see, Cheri and Amy are two of the bravest people I know. As far as memory serves, they have never jumped out of an airplane or sung a solo in public (two things I find to be equally terrifying). But they have done the hard soul work that comes with being who God has designed them to be.

A lot of authors talk about being fearless and brave. There are a lot of books with the not-so-subtle theme of "Just trust God and pull yourself up by your bootstraps, baby!" But this book you hold in your hand? This comes from the hard-won knowledge that a life lived with a focus of making others comfortable is a life of *less than*. And that's how Cheri and Amy lived most of their lives.

But . . . God . . .

Amy and Cheri invited God into the process of making each of them brand-new—and God continues the work in each of their lives. In miraculous, spectacular, only-God-could ways.

As you read this book, know one thing: You are not reading the work of a cheerleader standing on the sidelines. Amy and Cheri are on the field with you. Calling plays and taking hits. They are still in the game. They are the kind of authors—and people—I want to learn from.

And you, the reader? Thank you for doing the hard soul work of becoming who God created you to be.

I need you. The world needs you. Yes—even in all your you-ness. You are exactly what this world needs.

Kathi Lipp, bestselling author, *The Husband Project*
and *Clutter Free*

Introduction

It's 2:37 a.m., and she's wide awake.

Again.

Her busy brain is rehearsing everything she didn't get done today. All the things she's got to do tomorrow (which, she realizes with a new jolt of anxiety, is now technically *today*).

- *Rejoin that class at the gym. Swimsuit season is almost here . . . sigh.*
- *Be sure to swing by the dry cleaner's on the way home.*
- *Call the pharmacy first to make sure the prescription is really ready. (Can't afford a twenty-minute wait due to someone else's mistake today, of all days.)*
- *And for heaven's sake, whittle down the inbox and return Sharon's text!*

She tries to take slower, deeper breaths.

I've got to go back to sleep, or I'll be a zombie in the morning.

The mounting pressure in her chest squeezes a familiar question from her heart—a question she dodges during daylight hours. But every night, it tracks her down:

What's wrong with me?

"Just be yourself!" the adults in her life told her when she was little, as if being yourself was the easiest, most obvious thing in the world.

But she quickly figured out (a) it wasn't easy, and (b) they didn't really mean it. What they *really* meant was, "Be who we want you to be." So, at an early age, her motto became "Be all things to all people."

And did she ever get good at it.

It won her pats on the back, accolades galore, and a few plaques on the wall to boot.

Acquaintances consider her responsible, godly, efficient. Those who love her laud her as loving, cheerful, and productive—a real get-'er-done kinda girl! But behind her back they sometimes whisper, "Prickly, bossy, wound too tight, rigid."

Ask her about her relationship with God, and she'll tell you that she treasures it. But secretly, she struggles. She longs to do a better job of having consistent quiet time.

Watch her for a week, and you'll notice that she's fervent when she does spend time with God. She's sincere and really does want to experience more of God's presence and power in her day-to-day life.

She knows God offers freedom and joy. She believes God has given everyone gifts and a calling. She trusts that God is big enough to create change. But all these blessings seem to show up in other people's lives, not hers.

Instead of relishing an abundant life, she's drowning in an endless sea of meaningless "have-tos."

She does so much for so many, longing to be one of those legendary world changers, but she sees so little evidence that she's making any difference.

She feels anxious, overwhelmed, and (if she's honest) resentful toward everyone within a five-mile radius.

It's 3:03 a.m. now, and her mind still won't shut down. Like chocolates in the *I Love Lucy* scene with Lucy and Ethel in the candy factory,[1] the to-dos and anxieties never stop. They just keep coming faster.

1. If you don't recognize the reference, you're in for a laugh: https://www.you tube.com/watch?v=HnbNcQlzV-4.

And, as always, the inescapable question:

What's wrong with me?

If she sounds a lot like you, welcome to the club.

Who is she? She is me. She is you. She is a sisterhood who posts on social media in the wee hours, holding her breath to see if anyone else feels the same way.

You're not alone at 2:37 a.m. . . . or 3:03 a.m. . . . not by a long shot.

We've been there. (Maybe we should just give in and all do a group FaceTime next time?)

We know what it's like to feel so exhausted that the idea of adding one more thing to your to-do list will make your head pop off.

To feel responsible for All The Things, All The Time.

To cheerfully encourage others to "Choose joy!" while blinking back our own tears.

To believe that *generous* means "boundary-free."

To fear that it's selfish, even prideful, to learn about our gifts and strengths (let alone talk about them!).

We've been there. To be honest, sometimes we slip back for a visit. But we don't live there anymore.

You don't have to live there anymore, either. We're friends who have moved forward together and occasionally given each other a big ol' shove. Even though we may not have met you yet, we know this much about you, because it's been true about us:

Something's got to change.

You are created for less. Less worry, less over-attempting, less problem-preventing, less second-guessing.

You are created for more. More joy, more pure happiness, more fulfillment, more deep relationship.

God's delighted with us, friends, and He's so inspired by us that He sings over us. Scripture tells us that as we grew in our mothers' bellies, He was making plans for us that are good and that lead to an abundant life.

And, as crazy as this may sound, we know that when you truly invest in others, you'll receive more than you'll ever pour out.

But now we're running ahead of ourselves. So let's start here:

Something's got to change. And change is possible. We know it!

Not sure that's true yet? That's okay. It took a while to convince us, too.

There is a path that leads to a less draining, more fulfilled (but not more to-do) life. We've found a process that's changing our lives, and we're excited to share it with you.

We're here to equip you and cheer you on as you learn to . . .

. . . lose who you're NOT (Part 1).

. . . love who you ARE (Part 2).

. . . live your ONE life well (Part 3).

We know the pressure you're feeling now, the weight on your chest that makes it hard to breathe, but hold on and keep reading, sister.

There's an exhale coming.

Part One

LOSE WHO YOU'RE NOT

We invite you to join us on our journey of change. We sure aren't doing it perfectly, but we're learning that every failure offers a lesson. Journeys are so much better when you travel with friends. So won't you sign up for this road trip, even if you're still unsure?

We've got an amazing destination in mind, and it's got some great stops along the way:

- believing that God's best life is for us, not just everybody else
- embracing a growth mindset
- identifying and reveling in our gifts
- integrating our desires, our people's needs, and God's glory
- moving into a life of investing instead of spending

Doesn't that sound like a trip worth making? We promise it'll prove worth the effort.

The first step is a huge exhale, losing who you're *not*.

Releasing who you were never meant to be.

Letting go of what's weighing you down and holding you back.

So muster up your courage. Dust off your faith. Dig out your determination, and let's go!

one

You're Not Stuck Forever: So Celebrate Change

Amy

Change is . . . possible?

Wow. Pretty underwhelming, right? But that's the way I approached life for a long time. I wobbled between wanting change and being unconvinced that I could change. I'm a glass-half-full girl with sunshine in my pockets, and I'm always ready to toast your success. My belief in the transforming power of God for *you* is unshakable. But for me . . . well, my get-'er-done attitude and dangling to-do lists were wrapped around a quivering confidence, masking the doubt of whether I could ever get unstuck and earn God's best life for myself. (Hear the issues?!)

Not to mention that my natural tendency leans toward change-resistant. No matter how tough circumstances are, at least they're the life I know. It's the unknown, holding my breath as I dive into the deep, that's most scary. Curious about how we wrote the introduction about a woman lying in bed awake at 2:37 a.m.? Here's the scoop: Cheri gave me an inventory, a list of telling questions to answer, and the woman in the intro is basically me. If it's you, too, we're cut from the same cloth, but we need some change, sister!

A Moment to Choose

Over the Christmas holidays, a misunderstanding with a friend re-exposed all the issues I thought I had dealt with: expectations, over-planning, and a rigid attitude about how things "should be done." The evening started well with all the details falling into place. I hummed a tune while putting the finishing touches on dinner and the table. Some friends were coming to dinner, one set of new and one set of old, and I tingled with anticipation.

Suddenly my phone dinged, and my dear friend texted, asking me what time we were coming over. *What?* My mind spun in confusion. *They're supposed to be coming here*, I thought. I picked up the phone, calling her to straighten the tangle, but she was as confused as I was.

In the midst of multiple phone calls and texts to plan the time with our new neighbors, my friend and I had gotten our wires crossed. Her house was decorated and ready with food in the oven—just like mine! I was expecting her arrival at my house while she was expecting me to knock on her door any minute.

With irritation boiling below the surface, I asked her if I could think for a moment and call her back. Truthfully, my initial reaction wasn't great. *This is my party! After all this work—the planning, the cleaning, the cooking, the decorating—I want everyone at my house.*

Change is hard. There's no doubt about it. I've been a planner since I was small, joking constantly about my five-year plan while holding it tightly. I make my plans. I *love* my plans. I work my plans. Woe to anyone who messes with my plans.

But in that moment with my friend, I needed to find a new way to respond, a way that would grow the friendship instead of wreck it. I needed to change my way of reacting, and I knew I had to let go of my plans. Would I be able to do it? It was a moment of decision. I could stay stuck in my old ways or ask God for a new process to deal with my upended plans.

One Step at a Time

In my wrestling match to embrace a better way of living, I've realized there are two essential beliefs we have to grab and hold before change is possible:

1. We're created for empowered change.
2. Our failures are the beautiful (but sometimes painful!) steps toward change.

There's good news. Both of these essential beliefs for change are actually true. How can I state that with such complete confidence? The Bible tells me so.

One of the stories in Scripture that I've loved since I was little is the story of Zacchaeus found in Luke 19:1–10. Taking a fresh look at this riveting story has given me some mind-changing insights:

> Jesus entered Jericho and was passing through. A man was there by the name of Zacchaeus; he was a chief tax collector and was wealthy. He wanted to see who Jesus was, but because he was short he could not see over the crowd. So he ran ahead and climbed a sycamore-fig tree to see him, since Jesus was coming that way.
>
> When Jesus reached the spot, he looked up and said to him, "Zacchaeus, come down immediately. I must stay at your house today." So he came down at once and welcomed him gladly.
>
> All the people saw this and began to mutter, "He has gone to be the guest of a sinner."
>
> But Zacchaeus stood up and said to the Lord, "Look, Lord! Here and now I give half of my possessions to the poor, and if I have cheated anybody out of anything, I will pay back four times the amount."

Jesus said to him, "Today salvation has come to this house, because this man, too, is a son of Abraham. For the Son of Man came to seek and to save the lost."

Zacchaeus was definitely a man that needed a change. Verse 2 gives us a glimpse at two major character issues that left him stuck. First, he was the chief tax collector. In other words, he was sleeping with the enemy. The conquering Romans employed Jews to collect taxes from their countrymen to deliver to their Roman occupiers.

Not only that, but it was common practice for the Romans to allow these Jewish tax collectors to take extra money under the table. Based on the fact that Zacchaeus admitted his cheating ways and that he was rich, we can assume he was triply hated by the people around him. Tax collector. Strike one. *Chief* tax collector. Strike two. Rich. Strike three!

Zacchaeus was deeply flawed, but he must have had something new stirring within him. Something that made seeing Jesus worth running toward. Worth climbing a tree for. I love that Scripture says that he wanted to see "who Jesus was." Zach didn't just want to see what Jesus looked like. He wanted to know all about Him, watching His every move to gain an insight into His essence. The Jesus that Zacchaeus saw changed him, and the truths he experienced teach us truths about change.

Falling Short Doesn't Stop Us

Zacchaeus was short. We have shortcomings. Human limitations and flaws are just part of life, but they don't have to stop us. We don't have to stay stuck in them. What if Zacchaeus had said to himself, "Well, I'm short. It's just the way it is. It's the way I *am*. Guess I'll miss out on Jesus"?

I've taken that approach way too many times! Here's how it's gone in my head: *I'm a planner. It's the way I am, so I'm not changing plans.* Or, *I'm wired to want things a certain way, so I'll just have to endure exhaustion.* Or, *I want everyone to be happy, so I'll adjust my expectations to theirs even though I feel resentful.*

But Zacchaeus didn't use his height challenge as an excuse. Because he wanted Jesus so much—and because he wanted change so much—he found a way.

When we slow down to think about humanity, Zacchaeus's determination to get to Jesus is even more stunning. His unpopular vocation must have made him reluctant to face a hostile crowd. Surely he usually tried to avoid people's stares and comments and pointing fingers. Yet *nothing*—not his size or his unwanted presence—could keep Zacchaeus away from his pursuit of Jesus.

How tired are we of our current condition? How badly do we want change? How much do we want to live the better life Jesus has for us when we connect with Him? If we'll push aside all the obstacles and *run* to Jesus, He'll meet us with delight just as He met Zacchaeus. And not only will Jesus spend a few minutes chatting, like in this story, but Jesus will follow us all the way home, where real change starts to happen.

Change-Resistant People Can Be Overcome

In Zacchaeus's story there were people who criticized Jesus because they couldn't imagine a change in Zacchaeus. Sound familiar? In every life there are people who don't think we can change. Or they don't *want* us to change because it benefits them for us to stay stuck.

Zacchaeus shows us how to handle people who are resistant to our change. He tuned them out by focusing exclusively on Jesus. While the people were muttering, Zacchaeus addressed Jesus exclusively, "Look, Lord!" It makes me think of the lyrics to the classic hymn *Turn Your Eyes upon Jesus*, "And the things of earth will grow strangely dim in the light of His glory and grace." I can just imagine Zacchaeus making his declaration of change with his eyes *locked* on Jesus and the negativity of those around him bouncing right off. We love people, but when we're ready for change, we listen only to Jesus. Ultimately, we trust that the changes He makes in our lives benefit all those around us, too.

Jesus Is a Change Agent

Zacchaeus experienced a change—a miraculous change. He immediately and joyfully let go of the riches that had strangled him and took a cleansing breath of repentance, giving birth to a new life. Jesus was there, and He wasn't just a witness to Zacchaeus's change. He was the agent of Zach's change: the awesome power behind it.

Jesus empowers our change, too. He doesn't stand by and just watch to see how we'll do. When we climb down out of the tree of our self-made solutions and invite Him home, He pours out all that we need.

Jesus defines His role in this passage when He says, "For the Son of Man came to seek and to save the lost." Our Savior's saving isn't limited. Yes, it's there in the moment when we give our lives to Him at salvation, but the saving doesn't stop there. His restoring power continues through our whole lives, saving *all* that's been lost. Zacchaeus had lost his friends and his reputation, but when Jesus saved him, Zach received a life even better than the one it replaced.

Jesus saves our souls, and He wants to save other lost parts of us, too. Have you lost your peace? He wants to save it. Have you lost your purpose? He wants to save it. Have you lost your ever-lovin' mind? Jesus wants to save that, too! He's the source of the power we can't do without, and He's the Savior we need for empowered change. When we hand Jesus the broken pieces of our lives, He hands them back better than new. Jesus is just waiting for us to stop clinging to the tree.

What If I Can't Change?

This question is the root of most of our paralysis. If we don't try to change, then nothing seems lost. The real tragedy would be trying to change and finding out that we can't. Nothing would be more heartbreaking than such an outcome.

Here's the good news. Not only can we change, but God's created us for change and growth. I'm going to get a little geeky on you here. Brain scientists tell us that our brains function with neuroplasticity, a term that points to its meaning. Just as plastic can be reshaped, our thinking and actions can be altered because of the neuroplasticity of our brains. God has hardwired us for change.

That's established science, but we also need to be aware of our perceptions and belief patterns about our ability to change and grow. Stanford University psychologist Carol Dweck has defined our beliefs about change in two categories—fixed mindset and growth mindset. If you're a fixed-mindset girl (which I've been for most of my life), you see things in terms of either success or failure. There's no in-between. Growth mindset means that you see everything, even failure, as a learning experience with success occurring after many, many faltering steps toward growth.

My friend Glynnis Whitwer gave the best example leading to a flash of insight in my own life. She helped me see the silliness of my fixed mindset by saying, "Just think of a child learning to walk. They never fall and think, 'I'm not going to do that again!' They instinctively get up and try again. I like to think they are saying, 'Okay, I'm going to get myself back up, and I'm going to try to walk again.'"

Bing! All kinds of lightbulbs went on in my head when Glynnis described growth in terms of literal baby steps. Toddlers fall down innumerable times before they run across the floor. Babies listen for a whole year before they say a word. Change and growth happen on the inside for a long time before anything exhibits on the outside.

We're just the same. We can set aside our fear of trying to change by understanding that failure isn't the worst thing that can happen. It's part of growth. We can exhale, knowing that change only requires progress, not doing it all perfectly.

A Pilgrim's Progress

The night that my dinner plans went awry, I thought through options that would let me embrace a change, and I called my friend back with a revised set of plans.

"How about we make this a progressive dinner?" I asked my friend. "We'll walk around the corner to your house and bring our side dishes.

27

After eating the main meal at your house, we'll walk back to mine for coffee and dessert. What do you think?"

My friend loved the idea, so we set off on a short walk to spend a long evening basking in the company of friends. Our time together was even more fun than if we'd eaten at one house or the other. Our progressive dinner provided additional opportunities to enjoy the warmth of each other's homes and laugh about how easily miscommunication happens.

Jesus saved my soul forty years ago, but He's still saving and changing me. My past failures have been tools to teach me. That night He empowered me to hold back my hasty words and to implement an idea that saved a friendship.

Empowered by Jesus, I'm changing slowly but surely, and so can you. Feel free to let my confidence buoy you until you believe it for yourself.

Exhale. We can breathe easy, because change is possible!

☀ now breathe

Note: At the end of every chapter, Cheri and I will give you just one action step to keep it easy-breezy. We suggest reading the book slowly, too, so that these steps feel like blessings, not burdens. Purposeful progress is permanent progress!

Write down one way that you've grown in the last ten years. Take a few minutes thinking about what brought about that change in your life, and write a few sentences recording the catalyst or steps that led to positive change.

LOSE WHO YOU'RE NOT:

You're NOT permanently stuck.

Two

You're Not Exempt from Failure: So Join the Club. . . . We're All Members!

Cheri

Hi. I'm Cheri. And I'm a recovering perfectionist.

My membership in the 2:37 a.m. club goes all the way back to my teen years. I'd lie in bed, wide awake, analyzing my mistakes of the day and rehearsing my impending to-do lists for what felt like hours. Exhausted to the point of tears, I'd often crawl out from the covers, kneel face down on the floor, confess every wrongdoing I could recall, and beg God for forgiveness.

I can say "recovering perfectionist" because of a paradigm shift that began in my midforties. Come back in time with me to where it all began: at a leadership conference in a vast auditorium six years ago.

The conference schedule lists "9:45 a.m. General Session: Leadership As Improv." I suck in my breath, narrow my eyes, and stuff the program back in my computer bag.

I don't do improv. I like my spontaneity very carefully planned, thank you.

So I'll sit in the last row. And if anyone tells me to get on stage and "improv," I'll hightail it out the back door!

To my relief, the presentation turns out to be an improv jazz quartet. As the workshop begins, the leader discusses the difference between classical music and improv jazz.

Classical musicians are highly trained, skilled, and practiced performers. A classical musical score is detailed; each note is precisely shown. The purpose of performing classical music is duplication—doing what's been done many times before and doing it *perfectly*. The structure of classical music is set, even rigid.

With improv jazz, the musicians are also highly trained, skilled, and practiced performers. But the score is minimal. The purpose of improv is creativity, innovation, and dynamic change. In fact, the composer is the performer, and the music is being composed during the performance, giving it immediacy and vitality!

I am surprised to learn how much structure improv actually involves. But it is flexible, encouraging autonomy within community.

Then, the workshop leader says something so shocking, I can never recover from it.

"For us," he says, gesturing from the pianist to the saxophonist to the bass fiddler player to his trumpet, "errors are not a problem. In fact, we call errors 'competent mistakes.'"

I gasp.

Competent. Mistakes.

I comprehend the two words separately. My brain cannot make them work together. I convince myself that I've heard wrong, so at the break I march up and ask, "What was that you said about mistakes?" The leader laughs and repeats the phrase. Slowly, so I can write it down.

As I wrestle to wrap my brain around "competent mistakes," I realize that I've taken away a vastly different lesson from my own decade of classical piano lessons:

Mistakes mean only one thing to me.

Failure.

I started playing piano when I was five.

At first, I loved it.

I loved my teacher. I loved practicing. I loved getting better and better.

Then came my first recital.

When I sat down at the unfamiliar piano, I became *that* girl: the one you pity and dread, the one who fumbled, stopped, and started over.

And over.

And over.

The one who finally fled the stage (no reason to curtsey) and sat stoically through the rest of the recital until she could run home and cry.

My lessons continued until I was fifteen. Ten years of faithful practice and punch-in-the-gut performances. Ten years of knowing (or at least believing) I was a failure because I made so many mistakes.

Learning to Make Competent Mistakes

Over the weeks and months of pray-cessing what I learned at the Leadership As Improv workshop, I began to recognize how many of my daily choices were governed by an old, old rule that sounded a lot like this: *Nothing's worse than making mistakes; nothing's worse than failure.*

So this concept of competent mistakes represented a massive paradigm shift for me.

A mindset change, as Amy would say.

And while I'd love to report that the transformation was instantaneous—like the end of a Disney movie when dark, dismal gloom bursts into brilliant, beautiful joy—the truth is that it was slow. And hard.

I was used to working hard—really hard. But *allowing* myself (let alone *inviting* myself) to make so-called competent mistakes at work, in my relationships, and during my everyday life was a whole new kind of hard. For four and a half decades, I'd goaded and judged myself with Scriptures like Ecclesiastes 9:10, "Whatever your hand finds to do, do it with all your might," and Matthew 5:48, "Be perfect, therefore, as your heavenly Father is perfect. " Giving myself permission to mess up felt horrifying. Heretical. Like I was committing an unpardonable sin.

(Pardon me while I reach for one of the paper bags Amy and I hyperventilate into when the pressure starts rising. . . .)

As I was trying to figure out what it might look like to actually live out this competent mistakes concept, my friend Kathi Lipp asked me to contribute to a book she was writing. Honored, and thrilled by the possibility of fulfilling my lifelong dream of having my words published inside a book, I said yes on the spot.

And then I stalled.

I don't quite understand what she wants.

I stalled some more.

I don't think I can do the kind of writing she needs.

So I stalled even more.

With the deadline looming, I faced one of the scariest crossroads of my adult life: Would I work hard and expose myself to the criticism of a friend and her editors? Or would I keep doing what I'd been doing for months: *nothing*?

I thought ahead to when Kathi's book was released. I could open it up and find my words on the printed pages. Or I could open it up and see blank spaces—*nothing*—where my words could have been.

What if the pain of criticism stings for a few moments, while the joy of creation lasts forever?

I wrote five thousand words in two days, scared spitless every single second that I was writing garbage.

But for the first time in my life, I was more terrified of nothing than I was of failure.

Even though failure was possible, and certainly felt probable . . .

Instead of holding my breath . . .

I exhaled.

Nothing *Is* Worse

A few years later, I decided to take an improv class—the acting kind. But since I was still terrified of making mistakes (competent or otherwise!), I was thrilled to find improv instructors who also led a class in monologue: ten minutes on stage, all by myself.

Monologue included two appealing safety nets: a script and plenty of practice.

It was an eight-week class with two instructors and seven other students. Each week, we shared our working scripts, and then the eighth week was our performance.

As I shared with my classmates some of the poems and blog posts I'd written about my struggles with perfectionism, one man said, "It sounds like perfectionism is this street thug that's been beating the stuff outta you for your entire life!" (Only he didn't say "stuff.")

Another classmate, also a guy, said, "It sounds like perfectionism is the devil himself trying to steal your soul!"

Now, until I heard their feedback, I didn't realize how destructive perfectionism really was. It seemed so normal, like a quirky family friend that had been hanging around forever. I hadn't recognized how abusive Perfectionism had been to my mother, to me, and to my daughter, driving us like a taskmaster to work harder and harder and harder, never satisfied with anything we did. Or who we were.

In my monologue, I personified Perfectionism. I spoke directly *to* "him" and called him out for the crimes he'd committed, starting with how he'd brainwashed us to believe "Nothing's worse than making mistakes."

On the day of the actual performance, I was terrified. The last time I'd done drama was as a teenager, back when I had functioning memory cells. I was so afraid of (you guessed it!) *making mistakes.*

But something happened as I walked alone onto the dark, empty stage.

My fear of making mistakes was replaced by anger. A deep fury toward Perfectionism welled up, for all he'd stolen from my mother, from me, and from my teenage daughter.

It hit me: *Doing nothing is worse—far worse!—than making mistakes*

I'd taken a ruler on stage as a prop, just to give me something to do with my hands. (I have a chronic case of awkwardness.) That ruler soon became a symbol of Perfectionism's bad rules.

In the final moments of my monologue, I told Perfectionism in no uncertain terms, "You do not get my daughter, too!" and broke the ruler in half on behalf of every woman in my family who has been abused by this tyrant.

My performance that day was anything but perfect. My mouth was so dry from fear, I felt like I was choking on every word. I forgot my lines too many times to count. I even tripped over my own feet.

But as the crack of the ruler echoed over the audience, I discovered something glorious (and entirely unexpected) about finally breaking the bad rule of "Nothing's worse than making mistakes."

It feels really good.

Like you finally get to exhale.

Once you get started, you don't want to stop.

So you decide to finally host the dinner party you've been stalling on. Error terror shows up right on cue, ready to shut you down.

But you remember: *No more nothing. I'm gonna start taking baby steps. If I take a tumble, I'll chalk it up as a competent mistake, get back on my feet, and keep going . . . and growing.*

On the night of the party, when your smoke alarm reminds you that the garlic bread is done, you can tell yourself, "The bread may be burnt, but the company is good."

You exhale.

A few weeks later, you get invited to sing for church. You haven't sung in public for decades.

And you remember.

You remember the fun you all had at the dinner party. Even though (or especially because) you're now famous for your "Cajun" garlic bread.

You remember the fun before the fear.

You choose competent mistakes over doing nothing.

You take the baby step. You fall down. You get back up.

What If You're Better Than You Know?

I ended up loving the monologue class so much, I signed up for every session over the next several years, writing and performing six monologues. And after every single one, I drove home feeling the same way.

I felt bad.

But instead of believing I'd done bad because I felt bad, I remembered what my instructors taught me:

Feeling bad is part of art.

It's what happens when you get on stage and open yourself up to an audience. In fact, *bad* isn't even the right word. I was actually feeling *vulnerable.*

I wonder, now, if I was really as terrible at piano as I've remembered all these years.

What if I'd known that feeling "bad"–vulnerable, exposed, drained– after a performance is a perfectly normal part of making art?

What if I wasn't terrible after all? What if I was better than I thought? What if I was (dare I say) *good* at piano but never knew it because I felt so bad?

You know that meal you're sure you ruined? That conflict you keep replaying in your mind, wishing for a do-over? That moment at the microphone when you just wanted the ground to open up and swallow you?

What if your feelings aren't telling you about the end result—the food, the argument, the performance?

What if your feelings are telling you about the state of your heart after you gave the best you had? After you opened yourself up? After you were bravely *vulnerable.*

Despite how bad you may have felt, try asking yourself: *What if I really was better than I thought?*

Feeling bad while you're learning something new doesn't mean you did bad. Often, it's a signal that you're getting really good at making competent mistakes.

Whew!

What to Do When You've Blown It Big Time

What about those times when it's not just a competent mistake but a true failure?

My natural reaction is to try to hide the evidence. Avoid the people I've let down. Play pin-the-blame-on-someone-else. It's such an odd mix of pride and shame: I don't want to believe that I'm the kind of person who could do such a thing, and I'm desperate to keep others from finding out what I've done.

But I've been learning a better way from an unlikely role model: Peter. This story from Matthew has much to teach us about fear, faith, and failure.

> Shortly before dawn Jesus went out to them, walking on the lake. When the disciples saw him walking on the lake, they were *terrified*. "It's a ghost," they said, and cried out in fear.
>
> But Jesus immediately said to them: "Take courage! It is I. Don't be afraid."
>
> "Lord, if it's you," Peter replied, "tell me to come to you on the water."
>
> "Come," he said.
>
> Then Peter got down out of the boat, walked on the water and came toward Jesus. But when he saw the wind, he was afraid and, beginning to sink, cried out, "Lord, save me!"
>
> Immediately Jesus reached out his hand and caught him. "You of little faith," he said, "why did you doubt?"
>
> And when they climbed into the boat, the wind died down. Then those who were in the boat worshiped him, saying, "Truly you are the Son of God."
>
> Matthew 14:25–33, emphasis added

The disciples are cowering in fear, thinking Jesus is a ghost. When Jesus speaks, Peter not only recognizes His voice but responds to His words with immediate, audacious faith.

With his eyes on Jesus, Peter acts on Jesus's "Come" invitation by getting down out of the boat—leaving his fisherman's comfort zone—and walking on water.

Let's pause for a moment here. Yes, we all know what comes next. And I know that for recovering perfectionists, it's so tempting to discredit anything good when it's followed by disappointment.

But, y'all (Amy's rubbing off on me): Peter. Walked. On. Water. Just. Like. Jesus.

Jesus's voice transformed Peter's fear into an active faith that propelled Peter out of a bobbing boat and onto a lurching sea.

When error terror makes you want to cower in the boat, remember: Jesus transforms abject fear into active faith.

Okay, now for the part perfectionists like to pounce on: Peter fails.

Scripture isn't clear about how Peter "saw the wind," but if this were me, I'd be looking back at the boat to make sure my eleven BFFs were watching me. I'd be expecting to see awe and admiration on their faces. I'd be thinking, *Why do they look dismayed? Why are they motioning for me to turn around? Wait! Where did this wall of water come from? Where is Jesus?*

And this is where it's so easy to think, *See? See? Peter failed! If he'd just stayed in the boat, he wouldn't have failed!*

But if Peter had stayed in the boat, he wouldn't know the speed of the words "Lord, save me!" springing from his heart.

If Peter had stayed in the boat, he wouldn't know the strength of Jesus's grip on his hand.

He wouldn't know, from personal experience, how intentionally Jesus rescues before reprimanding. (Something perfectionists often do in reverse. Jus' sayin'. . . .)

Jesus defines Peter's failure—which is our frequent failure, too—in His question, "Why did you doubt?" Which can also be read as, "Why did you waver?" or "Why did you hesitate?" Doubt. Wavering. Hesitation. They're the telltale signs of error terror.

Yes, Peter failed. But rather than staying stuck in Peter's failure, let's focus fully on Jesus's response: First, He pulls Peter up to stand next to Him. Then He holds his humbled hand. And together they walk on water back to the boat.

This story raises valuable questions:

- What if Peter had been too afraid of making a mistake to respond to Jesus's invitation of "Come"?
- What if I'd never dared step on stage for my monologues?
- What if you stay so steeped in fear that you stay in your boat and miss experiencing Jesus's power? The miracle of walking on water with Him?

Friend, when error terror makes you want to cower in your boat, remember this: Jesus transforms abject fear into active faith.

And when you find yourself in the midst of actual failure, exhale three words:

Lord, save me.

He'll take you from there.

now breathe

Brainstorm what "Come" might look like for you. Pick one way, write it down, and practice it today. Tomorrow, reflect on your experience and pray-cess whether to repeat it or pick a new practice to try.

LOSE WHO YOU'RE NOT:

You're NOT required to be perfect.

three

You're Not Responsible for the World: So Roll the Elephant Off Your Chest

Amy

When I look at pictures of myself in my early thirties, I don't recognize myself. I look like a wannabe model for L.L.Bean. For all of you who love chinos and cable knit, please don't take offense. L.L.Bean is classic, but it's not *me*. I lean toward funky and quirky, so where did that woman who looks like me come from in her khakis and slip-on shoes?

Not only my wardrobe was baffling. Even reading my own emails, notes, and letters from that decade confuses me. I sound like my mentor—an amazing woman—but my sense of whimsy is missing, and I'm trying way, way too hard to be a spiritual giant. My clothes and my words were an external indicator of an internal wrestling match.

Just as I was walking into my calling to minister to women, my truest self stumbled off the path and got lost. It wasn't all bad news, though. Some aspects of my life made me the happiest I had ever been. Saying yes to being women's ministry director at my church launched me into a setting where my embryonic gifts of leadership and teaching came alive, and my inner extrovert thrived in the mix of being engaged in so many women's lives.

In some ways I flourished, but I also withered. The weight . . . oh, the weight.

Heavy expectations sat like Dumbo's mama on my chest, diminishing my ability to fill my lungs with freedom. My overdeveloped sense of responsibility needed to present as an exemplary leader, wife, and mom, attempting the impossible feat of being all things to all people. So I started to act the part. Speak the part. Dress the part—Fair Isle sweaters and all.

Sadly, the more I strove to rise to meet external expectations, the deeper I sank.

In looking back through the lens of two decades of maturity and hard-won wisdom, I wonder. What would have happened if, instead of caving to others' expectations, I had been my truest self in my calling? What parts of my calling weren't fulfilled at all because others' agendas hijacked my to-do list? And maybe most importantly, was I truly responding to what others expected and wanted, or were those just perceptions that I created myself?

Needs and Necessities

No matter what setting consumes our days, we have people around us that truly need us. There are co-workers who call for our insights and support. There are parents who deserve our attention and care. We have neighbors, Sunday school sisters, and committee members who require their share of us. There may be a husband who desires our love and respect or children who need us to wash their underwear and nurture their hearts. If you're single, there may be people who express their desires about the relationships you do or don't have, and we all have internet "friends" who are weighing in by displaying their highlight reels, their own version of what's right.

Sometimes the list of people who need us can feel overwhelming, especially if their expectations start to chip away at our time, our sense of self, or our calling. Here's a question to do a little assessment:

When you lie awake at night thinking about your list of tasks, who put those tasks there? God, you, or someone else?

Our connections require commitments, and that's not a bad thing. But as women, we often cross over into taking anything others hand us. What they expect of us. What they want us to do for them. How they want us to feel.

Sometimes that's okay and sometimes it's not.

It's not okay that I abdicated my personality to be who I thought others wanted me to be. It's not okay that I didn't bring my truest self to the assignment God had given me. It wasn't okay for my soul, and it wasn't okay for the people I loved and served. I almost suffocated under the weight of others' expectations and the ones that I carved in my own heart and mind.

When I honestly examine my heart without flinching at the hard truths, I know that the fault of letting others' tasks and expectations push out the life I'm created to live lies with me.

We're the only ones who can hold the line of our own lives, and there's a negative process that I see happening over and over through seasons of my life:

1. There are two kinds of expectations on me: legitimate or appropriate needs that people have for me and expectations put on me that aren't mine to shoulder at all.
2. I take on both kinds without examination.
3. On top of those, I heap my own list of I-should-bes and I-should-dos.
4. I begin to crumble under the mountain of expectations that are a mix of reasonable, unreasonable, and self-made.

Not good, right? We've got to learn to tease these apart so that we can narrow down.

- What's a reasonable or appropriate expectation, duty, or calling? These stay.
- What's an unreasonable or inappropriate expectation? These go.
- What's an expectation that I've generated based on what I *think* others want from me? These definitely go!

Plates of Trash and Other Quandaries

My friend Amber had a difficult relationship with a relative. As she was navigating the deep waters of improving that relationship, Amber had a realization in the form of a funny word picture.

"Sometimes my relative hands me a plate of trash," Amber told me. "My whole life I've accepted the plate she's handed to me as if I now actually own it, saying, 'Of course I'll take your trash. *Thank you* for this plate of trash!' Now, things have changed. I lovingly hand the plate back and sweetly say, 'Oh. You handed this to me, but it's not mine. This is *your trash* to hold or throw away.'" The picture Amber painted made me laugh, but it's perfect to help us as we deal with outside tasks, duties, attitudes, and demands that are passed to us. Sometimes we might have to hand the plate of trash back to the wrong-thinking part of ourselves!

Just this week, I had a job delegated to me by a well-meaning person at church. Simply reading the email with the details of the job made my chest hurt, so I knew I needed to pay attention to my reaction. In the past, I would have feigned cheerfulness, accepted the plate/job that was handed to me, shoved it into my already full schedule, and ended up resentful because I had to ditch something I felt called to in order to complete the task I'd been handed. A task that clearly belonged to someone else, not me.

But I didn't do that this time because I've been learning from Jesus.

Great Expectations

There's no other person in history who has had more expectations flung at Him than Jesus. He's the Messiah, after all. The Messiah was long-awaited, much-anticipated, and erroneously but well-defined in people's minds. His culture's expectations were a sampler plate of right and wrong standards. They anticipated a king who brought about an earthly kingdom, but the longer Jesus ministered, the more disappointed some of His followers became—including His cousin and friend John the Baptist.

Luke 7:18–23, 33–35 is an arresting picture of how Jesus handled what others expected of Him with a firm grace. In verse 20, John sends a question to Jesus through two of his disciples. "Are you the one who is to come, or should we expect someone else?" What a stunning question from the one who had paved the way for Jesus and baptized Him in the Jordan with God the Father and God the Spirit attending!

Where in the world did John's question come from? John started looking for some*one* else because he was expecting some*thing* else. Even at Jesus's crucifixion, the end of His life, people were trying to affix "king" to the sign on the cross above Him. John, a Jew, must have been wondering, like many others, *Where is the king we expected? Where is the military leader who overthrows our oppressors?* Maybe he even thought, *Where is the powerhouse Messiah that can spring me out of this prison?* Disappointment invaded and then doubt conquered.

One of the layers I've added to my study of the gospels is to consider Jesus's humanity, His feelings, and His reactions. When I put myself in Jesus's shoes here, it's painful. It feels rotten to have someone we love voice doubt and disappointment in us.

But Jesus didn't react to unreasonable expectations the way I've reacted. He wasn't angry and defensive, nor did He acquiesce, trying to fulfill someone else's agenda. Instead of Jesus shifting His calling, He gently helped John to shift his expectations. Jesus replied, "Go back and report to John what you have seen and heard: The blind receive sight, the lame walk, those who have leprosy are cleansed, the deaf hear, the dead are raised, and the good news is proclaimed to the poor" (Luke 7:22).

All along, Jesus had been proclaiming His mission.

From the book of Isaiah, Jesus proclaimed it in the temple: "The Spirit of the Lord is on me, because he has anointed me to proclaim good news to the poor. He has sent me to proclaim freedom for the prisoners and recovery of sight for the blind, to set the oppressed free, to proclaim the year of the Lord's favor" (Luke 4:18–19).

Jesus was crystal clear about His calling, and He was immovable. Gently He listed the proofs of His ministry to remind John of The Goal. Then Jesus unapologetically called John to come into alignment. "Blessed is anyone who does not fall away on account of me" (Luke 7:23 NLT). Without detouring, pursuing John with promises of change, or creating a clever new plan, Jesus held His course.

"Blessed is anyone who does not fall away on account of me." Within His parting sentence, there's a gentle rebuke *and* an engaging invitation to John. Jesus will not leave His path for John, but He beckons John to walk with Him. *Ouch!* And *How sweet!*

Only Follow the Father

When it's oh-so-tempting to attempt a trail that someone wants us to blaze, whether it's a task, a timetable, or a trade-of-self, we need to assess and then trust. If we decide that it's a trail established by the Father, we should follow it, knowing that it's good both for us and others.

But if it's *not* our given path, we shouldn't travel it no matter how much anyone else thinks we should. We need to trust that following our Father benefits *everyone* even when it leaves someone temporarily in a snit. People may well doubt our commitment to them and be disappointed in us. But in the end, detouring from our calling won't really bring the happiness to others that they thought we could give them.

Just think. It might have made John happy for a moment for Jesus to act more "Messiah-ish," but following John's plans would have kept Jesus from fulfilling His mission, ultimately leaving John without a Savior.

Jesus didn't accept every "plate" that was handed to Him. If the assignment matched His calling and what the Father had spoken to Him, then He accepted it. If the expectation didn't fit, He gently rejected it, reminded people of His calling, and continued doing what He was destined to do.

In our journey to lose who we're not, we have to jettison all people-pleasing that supersedes our desire to please God. If I get down-and-dirty honest, the unbalanced desire to please others is what causes the crushing weight of inappropriate expectations. A Father focus helps me to deflect wrong expectations rather than heap them on my weary back.

Whether it's the co-worker who wants to dump the group project into your solo hands, the mother who wants you to operate on her unreasonable time line, or the child who wants you to pay to fix the disaster he created, we need some skills learned from Jesus to know how to respond. We need Him to show us when to help and when "helping" is a well-disguised ploy for people-pleasing—a detour from following the Father.

Taking cues from Jesus helped me to handle the over-the-top email from church in a much different way than I would have in the past.

Evaluate the Expectation

When I first received the directions for overseeing a project at church, my knee-jerk reaction was to scramble to make it happen. Only when I paused did I start to ask myself these questions:

- Does this fit with what God has called me to do?
- Will I have to discard some of the activities I've already assessed and committed to do?

- Will agreeing to this project set a precedent for more unsolicited assignments in the future?

There's a definite starting point with these questions. To answer each question, we must be mindful of our mission. We must have set a charted course. We must be confident in our calling.

I know that may be a sticking point for you. That's okay. By the end of this book, you'll have a compass to find your true north. By now you can see, though, that without a clear sense of calling, it's easy to conform to others' expectations whether they're reasonable or not.

If a request falls within our calling, then fulfilling it will add to our purpose *and* truly help the other. That's the definition of an appropriate expectation.

It's the inappropriate expectations that we need to lose. These are outside of our God-given responsibility, and fulfilling these will divert us from our true calling and ultimately *hurt* the one we think we're helping.

Before we can decide whether to meet someone else's expectation for the use of our time, energy, money, or position, we have to correctly assess it. Knowing that it's appropriate helps us to move forward, but finding that it's inappropriate allows us to give an empowered no and shifts the weight of the expectation off of us.

Administrating the project at church didn't fit into the calling God has currently given me, so I was able to send back my no to the request with a clear conscience. Happily, I knew I could play a smaller part in this situation. Instead of taking on the whole project as requested, I responded that I'd be glad to commit a set number of hours to volunteer.

These days, I've found myself again by seeking the voice of my Father. I hear the other voices around me, and I love them. I consider them, but I don't follow them. I know it's weird to say that my quirky clothes and solo dance parties in my living room are evidence that I'm learning to exhale, but it's true. I'm pursuing God in a way that gives me the power to say yes and the power to say no as I add to my list. It allows me to lose who I'm not, letting God (and nobody else) define me—funky earrings and all.

☀ *now breathe*

Start a cumulative list of all the tasks in your life. (This will take a while, so add to it as you're able.) Take time to evaluate each one carefully, and put a star by the ones that are inappropriate or unreasonable. Today, choose one task with an unreasonable expectation attached to it, explain your calling to the person who holds it, and give that person a confident "no."

Write a prayer to God expressing your trust that He will bring good to that person.

LOSE WHO YOU'RE NOT:

You're NOT responsible for everyone all the time.

four

You're Not Defined by Your Past:
So Lose Those Old Labels

Cheri

When I was four years old, my brother held up a bright red bottle and said, "Hey, Cheri, would you like to try a drink of cherry juice?"

Now, I was a trusting little sister who adored her big brother and desperately wanted his approval. So I said, "Yes! I would love to try your cherry juice!"

Unfortunately, I was too young to know that T-A-B-A-S-C-O does not spell *cherry*. I took a huge gulp from the bottle, expecting to taste sweetness, only to feel fire in my throat, nose, even ears.

This is my earliest memory of betrayal.

Which I have *never* let my brother live down. When we get together for a meal, I surround his plate with Tabasco sauce bottles. I include at least one when I wrap his Christmas gift. For his fiftieth birthday bash, I wrote a silly poem blaming him for everything that's ever gone wrong in my entire life. Can you imagine how thrilled I was to rhyme "Tabasco" with "fiasco"?

He burned me when I was four, and I've been roasting him with that memory ever since.

But we know that not all hurts end up with funny endings.

When I was fifteen years old, my best friend, Tracie, decided she was done with me. I never knew why; one day we were Best Friends Forever, and the next she wouldn't speak to me.

A mutual friend asked her, "Don't you feel bad losing your friendship with Cheri?"

Tracie responded, "I'm not losing anything. I'm throwing her away, 'cause that's what you do with trash."

This is my pivotal memory of rejection.

The words "I'm throwing her away" left me struggling to breathe in the moment and put a stranglehold on my heart for decades.

I have a habit of ruminating on hurtful words I've heard, rehearsing them again and again in my head. Not on purpose, of course. It just gets stuck on automatic replay in my head, repeating the same hurtful words over and over.

And here's the kicker: What I hear, I take to heart.

So decades ago, I heard "I'm throwing her away" and took to heart *I am trash.*

I was well into my forties before I recognized the long-term impact of the hurtful words that get stuck on repeat. Even though my body was four decades old, in many situations I still talked and thought and reasoned like a girl.

A girl gripped by fear.

I feared betrayal. At the slightest sign of disloyalty, I'd internally cringe: *Oh no, not again.*

I feared rejection. When I noticed even a hint of disapproval, I'd tense up: *Here we go again.*

Most of all, I feared the panic triggered by other people's wounding words that echoed in my head and heart. *Again and again.*

I didn't want to stay stuck as a girl gripped by fear. I didn't want my past to define me. I *wanted* to find freedom!

But I didn't know how.

The Echo of Old Voices

A little girl still lives in each of our hearts, and she has a hard time forgetting the hurtful words she's heard.

After all, what we hear, we take to heart. Old voices linger, yammering away on automatic replay:

"Who do you think you are?"

"Do you really think you have something of value to offer?"

"Why would anyone listen to you?"

Maybe, like me, you look in the mirror at a woman who is decades old, but you find that in many situations you still talk, think, and reason like a girl.

A girl gripped by fear.

What labels do your fears wear?

Those who were supposed to help ended up hurting you. So now, you hyperventilate in hypervigilance.

Oh no, not again.

You've been discarded before. So now you're holding your breath, just waiting for the inevitable.

Here we go again.

You hear those same old words over and over, and you take them to heart even as they wring it empty of joy.

Again and again.

You don't want to stay stuck as a girl gripped by fear. You don't want the past to define you. You want to find freedom!

But you don't know how.

How Jesus Moves Us beyond Our Past

Early in His ministry, as recorded in John 4:4–42, Jesus encounters a woman who is defined by her past. While traveling through Samaria, He sits down, on His own, by Jacob's well. When a lone Samaritan woman comes to fill her jar with water, Jesus asks her for a drink.

Her response is revealing.

"You are a Jew and I am a Samaritan woman. How can you ask me for a drink?"

In other words, "Dude, you're asking the wrong gal."

Perhaps she's thinking, *Once he recognizes his mistake, he'll back off and leave me alone.*

It's a classic self-protection strategy: *I'll reject you before you reject me.*

But Jesus does the exact opposite. Instead of distancing, He demonstrates how intimately He knows her.

"Go, call your husband and come back," Jesus tells her.

"I have no husband," the woman replies.

Jesus says, "You are right when you say you have no husband. The fact is, you have had five husbands, and the man you now have is not your husband. What you have just said is quite true."

The woman is stunned to discover that Jesus knows "everything" she "ever" did.

For her, "everything I ever did" comes down to her many failed relationships.

We women tend to define ourselves by our relationships. As a child, I defined myself as John's little sister, Tracie's best friend. I became Daniel's wife and then Annemarie and Jonathon's mother. Physically, I grew up. But emotionally, I still defined myself by my relationships.

And it's dangerous when "everything I ever did" is defined by our relationships with other people. We become vulnerable to betrayal, to rejection, to holding others' hurtful words in our hearts.

Because of this woman's many failed relationships, hurtful words echo in her heart, as well:

"Who do you think you are?"

"Do you really think you have something of value to offer?"

"Why would anyone listen to you?"

Jesus boldly contradicts these old wounding words by engaging "the wrong gal" in one of the deepest discussions of theology recorded in all of Scripture.

When she says, "I know that Messiah . . . is coming. . . . He will explain everything to us," Jesus's reply is unexpected and uninhibited.

"I, the one speaking to you—I am he."

Jesus responds to the facts about who she is by revealing the truth of who He is.

To the woman whose mission is protecting her tender heart from feeling betrayed *again*, rejected *again*, criticized *again*, Jesus is candid, vulnerable, and utterly authentic.

For the first time in years, she senses that it's safe to let down her guard. To exhale with a very long sigh of pure relief.

But then, like her worst fears showing back up right on cue, Jesus's disciples return.

Although nobody actually says, "What do you want?" or "Why are you talking with her?" everyone knows what everyone else is thinking . . . even though nobody says anything out loud.

Can't you hear their self-righteous sniffs of indignation? They only see her labels: *Samaritan. Woman. Sinner. Slut.* They're silently seething, dying to say,

"Who do you think you are, talking to Jesus?"

"Do you really think you have something of value to offer Him?"

"Why would He listen to anyone like you?"

The odds aren't in her favor: twelve condescending men versus one outcast woman.

So she leaves. But not in reaction to them. She leaves because of her response to Jesus. He's transformed her, and she knows exactly what she needs to do. *Now.*

Running back to town, she doesn't know that she's about to become the first evangelist. She has no clue that she is going to literally bring people to Christ so they can hear for themselves and "know that this man really is the Savior of the world." She hasn't even done what she went to the well to do!

All that matters right now is that she's become someone new. She's rejected others' labels and accepted Jesus as her Savior.

John 4:28 (NLT) gives us this breathtaking detail about the change Jesus has already made in her: "The woman left her water jar beside the well and ran back to the village."

See who she's become?

A woman who leaves her jar at the well.

Can't you just imagine her running pell-mell back into town, her heavy jar left behind with Jesus?

Now ask yourself: *What would it be like to be a woman who leaves her jar at the well?*

After all, you know what it's like to go to the well at noon alone. You have your own experiences of betrayal, rejection, and criticism that make you feel labeled, different, isolated, even shunned.

So you carry that heavy jar full of fears from your past all by yourself.

You've carried it for so long, you know just how to balance it: how to hold your head up, how to tighten your grip, how to suck in your gut, how to throw your shoulders back, how to take your next step.

But oh—go ahead and heave that sigh—how you long to be a woman who leaves her jar at the well!

To encounter Jesus and leave it all with Him.

It's not that the past doesn't matter, but now something new matters more.

When the Samaritan woman leaves her jar at the well, she has heard and taken to heart Jesus's life-giving words.

She is no longer a girl gripped by fear; she is a woman held by faith.

Jesus offers this new identity to you, too.

No More Defining Moments

> When I was a girl,
> I talked like a girl,
> I thought like a girl,
> I reasoned like a girl.
>
> When I became a woman,
> I put my girlish ways behind me.
>
> 1 Corinthians 13:11,
> author's paraphrase

I don't know what causes you to feel like a girl gripped by fear.

But I do know that one of the most effective ways to put our "girlish ways" behind us is to take our defining moments to Jesus.

A defining moment is a pivotal past event that has a choke hold on you, influencing and even dominating your present life.

It's so easy for a single, short event from your past to become a defining moment that clings to you and controls you even now—without your awareness, let alone your permission.

And the fear provoked by defining moments can knock the wind out of you without warning.

The little girl part of your heart tries to cope with defining moments in one of three ways:

1. **Cover it up.** *I'll put on my happy face and move on as if it never happened.*
2. **Make up for it.** *I'll work hard to prove "them" wrong, to please and appease.*
3. **Give up.** *The past can't be changed, so why should I bother?*

There's only one way to put these girlish ways behind you.

Show up at your well.

Jesus is already there, just waiting for you.

He knows all about your fears.

He knows you.

And He longs to reveal himself to you, as the redeemer of your past, comforter in the present moment, and creator of your future. Invite Him to rewrite the stories you tell yourself about your past and prepare to be amazed.

While you can't undo what was done or said, Jesus can lead you to review the past, giving you new insights that lead to deeper understanding.

A few years ago, I started taking my defining moments to Jesus. As I pray-cessed those hurtful words—"I'm throwing her away, 'cause that's what you do with trash"—that had haunted me for so many years, the Holy Spirit spoke to my heart.

It wasn't about you. Those words came from her own pain and broken-ness. They were never about you.

And He reminded me of things I'd forgotten.

The empty bottles in and around Tracie's house. The holes in the walls. The sunglasses she wore on cloudy days and the long sleeves when it was sweltering.

As I saw Tracie anew through the eyes of compassion, that defining moment was put into perspective and its power over me was broken.

Those words no longer play through my head or my heart. They no longer define me.

As you take your defining moments to Jesus, you come to realize that there is no such thing as "a defining moment."

Nothing in your past defines you.

You are defined by Him.

No one else.

Jesus shows you who He is so you know who you are.

Not who those defining moments say you are. Not who you once were.

But who you really are.

With Him.

Show Up and Grow Up

Fears from the past will keep cropping up as long as we're on this earth. But we don't need to panic. They're no cause for hyperventilating, for fight or flight.

We can breathe easy, knowing that fears from the past don't mean that we don't have enough faith. "Such love has no fear, because perfect love expels all fear. If we are afraid, it is for fear of punishment, and this shows that we have not fully experienced his perfect love" (1 John 4:18 NLT).

Whenever you feel afraid, it simply means you need to experience more of God's perfect love. We don't need to cover up our past, make up for our past, or give up because of our past. We simply need to show up at the well. Show up to hear His words and take Him to heart.

The more we show up, the more we grow up.

Our fears from the past need not define us. Jesus waits at the well. He shows us who He is so we can know who we are.

We are no longer girls gripped by fear.

We are women held by faith!

☀ now breathe

Print a copy of your favorite childhood photo of yourself. Frame or mount it so there's a border (at least one inch), and write, "I am no longer a girl gripped by fear; I am a woman held by faith!" around the photo. Display it as a prominent reminder that when fear shows up, you need to meet Jesus at the well. (Pre-designed borders for all sizes of photos are available to download and print at ExhaleBook.com!)

LOSE WHO YOU'RE NOT:

You're NOT defined by old labels.

five

You're Not a Country without Borders: So Draw Healthy Lines

Amy

I gasped as I saw the list of grades on my computer screen. The truth was there in black and white. Those shocking letters reflected the fact that my husband, Barry, and I had been investing *far more* hard work to earn the money to send our son to college than he had been investing in his classes.

I was furious, but my initial reaction was to throw up my hands and avoid a confrontation. *It's his life,* I thought. *He'll just have to deal with the natural consequences.*

Moving in the surplus energy of my anger-induced adrenaline rush, I headed outside to work in the yard. I hacked away at an ornamental tree, trimming extra branches that had sprouted outside of its natural shape, all the while muttering and wiping sweat caused by the southern heat from my eyes.

As I pruned, my frustration began to quiet, and God began to speak. "Amy," He whispered to my heart, "aren't you glad I haven't given up on you? I've never thrown up my hands when you headed in the wrong direction or asked too much. I've pruned you because I love you."

My eyes filled with tears as I remembered the times God has set boundaries for my protection, and I prayed as I worked.

How do we say "no more" in a loving way, Lord?

How do we get him to see the reward in work?

Where should the lines be?

What if he's mad?

What if he ignores us?

Questions and doubts filled my head, but I knew that I couldn't wash my hands of the problem, so I headed in for a spousal consult in order to set some healthy boundaries of our own.

Jesus Is Our Exhibit A

I have a Bible with fonts in two colors, and you probably do, too. Over the decades, I've come to love every word in Scripture, but I'm particularly enamored with the words in red—Jesus's words.

Recently, I realized that all the words in red start at the beginning of Jesus's ministry, when He was an adult, except in one place, the Gospel of Luke. This is the only story recorded in Scripture of Jesus as a preteen, the space where humans swing between childhood and adulthood.

Every year Jesus' parents went to Jerusalem for the Festival of the Passover. When he was twelve years old, they went up to the festival, according to the custom. After the festival was over, while his parents were returning home, the boy Jesus stayed behind in Jerusalem, but they were unaware of it. Thinking he was in their company, they traveled on for a day. Then they began looking for him among their relatives and friends. When they did not find him, they went back to Jerusalem to look for him. After three days they found him in the temple courts, sitting among the teachers, listening to them and asking them questions. Everyone who heard him was amazed at his understanding and his answers. When his parents saw him, they were astonished. His mother said to him, "Son, why have you treated us like this? Your father and I have been anxiously searching for you."

"Why were you searching for me?" he asked. "Didn't you know I had to be in my Father's house?" But they did not understand what he was saying to them.

Then he went down to Nazareth with them and was obedient to them. But his mother treasured all these things in her heart.

Luke 2:41–51

In every other gospel the story skips from baby to man, so this passage is a fascinating glimpse into Jesus's understanding of His mission. It's also a story that sheds a bright light on how to approach our own boundaries when they conflict with the needs, wants, and preferences of others. Jesus shows us the way when expectations and relationships get sticky.

About Our Father's Business

Let's recap this segment of Jesus's story: The Holy Family—Joseph, Mary, and Jesus—had a holy habit. Every year they followed God's law and trekked to Jerusalem to celebrate Passover. We don't know if Jesus accompanied them on all the previous trips, but we know for sure that He went the year He turned twelve.

In a Bible story that sounds a lot like a pop-culture movie plot, Mary and Joseph were a full day's journey along the road home following the celebration when they realized their son wasn't with them.

Mary and Joseph were alarmed when they discovered Jesus missing. Scripture tells us that they turned right around, returned to Jerusalem, and searched for Him for *three full days*.

Let's pause here a moment. If you've ever been in charge of a child and lost her, even for a moment, you know the panic. Three whole days? We're talking missing persons reports and an Amber Alert.

Three days of looking means that the temple, where they ultimately found Him, wasn't Mary and Joseph's starting point. Scripture doesn't tell us where they looked, but high-and-low probably sums it up. Maybe like the rest of Jewish culture, they expected to find Jesus, the Messiah, near the palace consulting with rulers rather than sitting in the temple courts with religious leaders.

If they had truly understood Jesus's purpose, they would have searched the temple first.

Jesus's parents were evidently a little fuzzy about His mission, but He wasn't confused at all. He was clear and compelled by it. "'Why were you searching for me?' he asked. 'Didn't you know I *had to be* in my Father's house?'" (emphasis added).

The New King James Version translates His second question in a way that I love: "Did you not know that I must be about My Father's business?"

"About My Father's business . . ." Now, that's a clarifying idea. What does it mean to be about our Father's business, and how would purposefully finding our Father's moment-by-moment direction make our lives different?

Too often I live life by the seat of my pants. My gargantuan to-do lists, my texts, my voicemails, and my growling tummy dictate what's next rather than intentional thought on my part. I default to the next "important" thing in front of me, but Jesus never did.

Later in His ministry, Jesus explained His mission mindset this way: "I do nothing on my own but speak just what the Father has taught me. The one who sent me is with me; he has not left me alone, for I always do what pleases him" (John 8:28–29). In other words, Jesus only spoke what His Father told Him to speak. He only did what His Father told Him to do. I've come to think of this as the Principle of Intention, and you can follow it all the way through the gospels. Jesus cared immeasurably for others, but His Father's directions superseded everything else.

Being about our Father's business means that we live through the Principle of Intention, too. We say the words our Father is telling us to say and not one word more. (Can a chatty girl just insert a "MERCY!" right here?) We do the things our Father is telling us to do and not one iota more. God's directions become our boundaries.

As Jesus sat in the temple engaging with the teachers, He was about His Father's business, doing and saying what He'd been told. Because Jesus had submitted himself to the limitations of time and space, He wasn't able to be both in the temple and with His parents on the way home. And there's the rub.

When Others Get Up in My Business

You've probably experienced the same thing Jesus ran into over and over again in His life. You've intentionally chosen to follow the Father, but somebody in your life isn't happy. Your choice has stepped on their preferences, and it looks like feathers are going to fly.

Just listen to Mary here. The wayward child is found, and suddenly it's zero to sixty. Based on my experience, the tone I'm hearing in my imagination when Mary says, "Son, why have you treated us like this?" is high-pitched and louder than usual. She's not a happy mama. Nobody likes to be on the receiving end of disapproval, so I can imagine that Jesus, in His humanity, felt a little uncomfortable, too.

If you're like me, this is the point where you tend to fold like a house of cards in a gale. When a friend recently doled out undue criticism about a mutual friend, I was silently complicit instead of listening to my Father's whispers to defend the truth. But Jesus wasn't silent, and He didn't apologize. He explained, "I had to be in my Father's house." Jesus set a boundary based on His business and stood strong, and we can do the same. My Father's business is my boundary.

Can we pause and be honest here? Some of our loved ones won't *ever* understand when we set a boundary so that we can follow the Father. When people question our choices . . . When they want something we're not called to give . . . When our boundaries conflict with their desires, it can be excruciating, and that's when we need to trust God for the peace that He provides as we walk close to Him. It's when we have to "pass the plate back," just like I talked about in chapter 3.

Others will come around in time as Mary did when she once again "treasured all these things in her heart." Whether or not they ever acknowledge it, our people always benefit when we're living intentionally with one ear tilted in God's direction. He's just good like that. The overflow is that our hearts are delighted and we glorify Him.

Ahhhhh. Exhale.

Three Steps to Powerful Intention

Barry and I set about our Father's business as we dealt with our son and his grades. We sought to set some healthy boundaries by walking through the steps of Jesus's Principle of Intention—steps that apply to every relationship, not just between parents and child.

1. **We listened for God's voice.** Before we sprang into action, we prayed for wisdom. We asked God to help us do the right thing.

2. **We did what God directed us to do.** After praying, Barry and I took action, implementing what we believe was an inspired idea. We wrote out a contract with the specifics of what we would and wouldn't do based on the outcomes of next semester's grades. We also addressed a few other areas where the train had run off the relational tracks.

3. **We said what God instructed us to say.** After making copies of the contract that all three of us could sign (I knew I'd have the temptation to chicken out at the end!), we had the hard conversation. I marveled at what a faithful provider God is

in every circumstance. Just weeks before, God gave us loving words for the line we drew in the sand. Cheri and I had interviewed Lori Wildenberg, author of *Messy Journey*, for *Grit 'n' Grace*; she gave us a kind but candid script to use with our adult children. In the moment of confrontation with our son, I heard her words tripping from my tongue. "Son," I said, "we love you. That will never change. You're ours, and we'll *always* love you unconditionally. But we will not *fund* you unconditionally."

Was our son happy in the moment? Did he hear the hard things with joy? No. That day and the next few weeks were painful for everyone. Barry and I had to focus on our hopes for the future, strive to stay emotionally connected to our son, and give God time to work.

Personally, I had to fight sinking into the what-ifs and slapping bad-mama labels all over myself, but I knew that was all water under the bridge. God bolstered me to courageously stand on a faith that vanquished my overdeveloped sense of responsibility. Scripture reminded me again and again that others' expectations don't dictate my duties. Instead, I leaned on God to use the boundaries He gave to propel my son back onto the path.

The Beauty of Boundaries

Our one glimpse into Jesus's childhood shows us that boundaries are biblical. Put simply, setting a boundary means choosing God's direction over someone's expectation. By living with the Principle of Intention, seeking God's direction for everything we do and say, we can find the lines that will preserve our time, our energy, our finances, and our sanity. It's simple but definitely not easy.

But is it worth it? Oh yes. I don't ever want to pretend that every package in our broken world ends up with a pretty pink bow, but Barry and I have gotten to see the benefits of boundaries with our son. A year later, we can see how our fiscal and relational boundaries have produced a result beyond what we could have dreamed. Our powerful, transforming God has been at work.

Our son could have responded to the contract and hard words by punching a hole in the wall or by leaving home. He could have raged or shut us out. Instead, he responded with humility and repentance. He accepted both our love and our discipline.

Two semesters after our contract was signed, he's enjoying the intrinsic reward of good grades won through hard labor. More important than good test scores, he's experiencing a deeper relationship with God, and he's sharing riveting stories of how God is personally guiding and directing him. His permission to share his story in this book so that others can grow is further proof of a huge maturing work.

I've experienced a long, cleansing sigh of relief. The lines I drew left a blessed space in my emotions and my mind that used to be filled with the clutter of unreasonable expectations. My bank account is enjoying the satisfaction of a great investment. My time is freed from one contentious conversation after another. This is the delicious fruit of turning away from my first impulse to wash my hands clean by passively avoiding a problem, taking responsibility on myself instead of directing it where it belonged. It's the lovely blossom of living the Principle of Intention.

We can let go of worrying that God's boundary lines won't be for our good or that they will leave our family, friends, or co-workers adrift. Jesus shows us that faithful following, even when it clashes with someone else's agenda, sets us in a place to enjoy God's glorious work. Work that ultimately benefits us and all those around us.

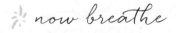

now breathe

Take time today to pray and ask God how He wants you to respond in the area that most needs a boundary. Sit in silence listening until you feel He's spoken. Then, live out the Principle of Intention. Do what He says to do and say what He says to say.

Note: God's directions never violate Scripture. If you're concerned that your action or words might not be biblical, pause for study before you act.

LOSE WHO YOU'RE NOT:

You're **NOT** *boundaryless.*

six

You're Not Really Wonder Woman: So Breathe a Sigh of Relief

Cheri

Daniel was in the midst of making blueberry pancakes when I decided to make an apple crisp.

I brought out the Granny Smith apples, my fancy peeler, a lemon, and the grater . . . all the while keeping one eye on what my husband was doing.

You know, in case he needed my help.

And boy, did he ever!

He's adding Bisquick to blueberry muffin mix? You can't do that!

He's rinsing the blueberries with hot water? He's going to ruin them!

He's making the batter that thick? He'll burn them for sure!

I sucked in my gut, clenched my teeth, and channeled all my will-power toward keeping my thoughts to myself.

Trying to look nonchalant, I sliced my apples, added lemon zest and juice, got a second bowl for the crumble topping, and measured out brown sugar and oats.

But when Daniel left the kitchen briefly, I could stand it no more.

I snuck over to his skillet, slipped a knife under one pancake, lifted it up to check, and gasped in dismay:

Black.

Just as I suspected!

When Daniel returned, I announced, "I *knew* I smelled something burning!"

Unfazed, Daniel rescued his burnt pancakes, turned down the heat, and poured a couple more on the griddle.

I returned to my apple crisp.

And immediately wondered, *Why are there oats all over my apples?*

Followed by, *What's all this brown sugar doing in with the apples?*

Oops.

In my hypervigilance over Daniel's baking, I'd lost focus on my own. Instead of measuring the oats and brown sugar into the second bowl, I'd dumped them in with the apples.

And started mixing.

So now my thin apple slices were stuccoed with gooey clumps of old-fashioned oats and globs of brown sugar.

During the twenty minutes I lost trying to salvage my mess, I tried to find someone to be mad at other than myself.

All that wasted time!

All those wasted materials!

All that wasted energy!

All because I'd forgotten a vital truth:

Help is only received as help *when the other person actually wants it.*

When I feel the urge to swoop in and save the day, but no one has actually said, "Hey, could you help me?" nine times out of ten it's Meddlesome Me rearing her controlling head.

The Problem with Living Hypothetical Lives

It can feel so satisfying to be the go-to person others turn to when they need a talented troubleshooter.

When we're following God's leading and living out of the natural and spiritual gifts He's given us, we can certainly offer guidance, teaching, and wise counsel.

But it's deceptively simple to convince ourselves that we're being servant-hearted problem solvers when we're actually being control-seeking *problem preventers*.

Does this sequence feel at all familiar?

1. You sense a possible problem long before it occurs.
2. You imagine all the negative consequences of #1.
3. You experience the emotional, physical, and even relational reactions of #2.
4. You develop multiple plans to prevent all permutations of #1.
5. You attempt to execute All The Plans—along with anyone who gets in your way.

I call this exhausting routine "living hypothetical lives."

Hypothetical lives are imaginary scenarios we concoct based on all the problems that *might* happen . . . problems that *could* happen . . . problems that we need to *prevent* from happening.

When we get caught up in living hypothetical lives, what started as true helping quickly morphs into meddling. And we start hyperventilating because we're running around desperate to fix one thing and stop another and prevent five others, only they keep multiplying so we run faster and faster, and soon we're gulping for breath until our chest burns from the insanity of it all.

Meddling chokes the life out of us and the love out of our relationships.

Confessions of a Problem Preventer

Scripture offers us a cautionary tale about a die-hard problem preventer whose choices and consequences teach us what not to do. Her story is found in Genesis 25–27. Here's what her story might sound like in her own words:

> My name is Rebekah. And I never meant to be a meddler.
>
> I didn't wake up one morning and decide, "I want to become a controlling wife and mother." None of us start out that way. We start out the way God created women: soft . . . comforting . . . flexible. Then decades pass. And one day we stare in the mirror, wondering, "How did I get so hard?"
>
> If you know my story, you know it started well enough . . . at a well, in fact. I had no idea I was auditioning for my future when Abraham's servant asked me for a drink and I offered water for his camels, too. I didn't know that I was a direct answer to his prayer.
>
> Prayer played such an important part in our early years. When I first saw my future husband, Isaac, he was praying. I soon learned that Isaac had a rich history with God. His experience on Mount Moriah taught him that God will provide.
>
> When I didn't get pregnant, he knew what to do: pray. Isaac prayed to the Lord on my behalf. Next thing you knew, I was pregnant and so excited! Until things felt wrong. There was so much movement, I was scared.
>
> Don't judge me for the question I asked. A more mature woman might have asked, "Is my baby okay?" I asked, "Why is this happening to me?" I know it sounds self-centered. But if you're honest, you'll admit you've asked the same question, too.
>
> "Why is this happening to me?"
>
> Have you ever thought to yourself, "If God would just tell me why, then I would trust Him fully?" Have you ever thought, "If God would just tell me why, then I would obey Him without question?" If He would just settle things, once and for all . . . answer this one question. How hard could it be for Him? And what a bargain! One answer in exchange for a lifetime of devotion.
>
> "If God would just tell me why, everything would turn out fine." Yeah . . . I thought the exact same thing. I went to God and asked Him, "Why is this happening to me?"

And I got my answer! God answered The Big Question for me! He told me why, in detail: two nations . . . two peoples . . . one stronger than the other . . . the older serving the younger. God gave me my why.

But everything did not turn out fine.

As our boys grew, my husband preferred Esau, while I loved Jacob.

But the truth is that long before we picked favorites from our children, I picked a favorite in my marriage. I picked Rebekah over Isaac-and-Rebekah. I picked myself over unity with my husband. I got my answer to The Big Question from God. He told me why, in detail.

But I didn't tell Isaac. I kept it to myself. For myself. Our boys didn't cause the split in our family. They were born into a gap. A gap that started when I misused the answer God gave me. A gap that had widened into a chasm by the time we each picked a favorite son.

Picking a favorite is the easy way out.

If I'd been more willing to learn to love Esau—my harder-to-love son—God could have stretched me, bent me, and molded me. Instead, I settled. For what came easily.

And the choice to settle produces the need to MEDDLE.

I meddled the day I heard Isaac tell Esau to hunt game, fix him food, and return for his blessing. Instead of praying, I took matters into my own hands. God had told me that the older would serve the younger, and I was going to make sure that it happened.

I never meant to be a meddler.

But I treated Jacob—a grown man—like a little boy. "Do what I tell you, and Mommy will fix everything. . . . Let the curse fall on me." What was I thinking?!

Worse yet, I *knew* my husband and my sons well. I knew what made them tick and what ticked them off. I knew just how to fix the tasty food Isaac loved. I knew exactly where Esau's best clothes were stored. I knew that Jacob's hands and neck were smooth. I knew my husband and my sons intimately, and I used my intimate knowledge of each man against him.

I never meant to be a meddler.

I never meant to be the kind of woman who used intimate knowledge as a weapon, who betrayed trust. But I became that kind of woman.

To meddle, you must betray trust. A lesson my son Jacob learned all too well. He used his intimate knowledge of his father's weakness—his blindness—against him.

I never meant for meddling to go this far. I cringe when I think of all of Jacob's lies:

"I am Esau." (*I'm actually Jacob.*)

"Your firstborn." (*Your second born.*)

"I have done as you told me." (*I've done what Mother told me.*)

"Please sit up and eat some of my game." (*Some of your own kid goats.*)

"So that you may give me your blessing." (*Before Esau gets back.*)

When Isaac asked, "How did you find it so quickly, my son?" Jacob replied, "The Lord your God put it in my path."

Oh, Jacob, you went too far! I never meant for meddling to go this far.

You evoked the most powerful moment in your father's history with God for your own personal gain. You suggested that God gave you the wild game just as He provided the ram on Mount Moriah. This lie—in the midst of a lie—desecrates your father's core truth: that God will provide.

My attempt to gain control spun even more wildly OUT of my control when Esau returned. "Bless me, too!" The cry of every boy to his father. At that point, I should have seen that my meddling had done far more damage than good. I should have confessed and repented. I should have sought forgiveness of my husband and sons. My meddling days should have been over.

But this is what happens with meddling: It takes on a life of its own.

And I was in this world of my own making where—crazy as it sounds now—I still thought I could fix everything. I was already busy with Plan B: "Now then, my son, do what I say. . . ."

All my plans failed. I still tried to fix everything. But once Jacob left, I never saw my son again.

How to Stop Being a Problem Preventer

Like Rebekah, we can be so convinced that we are the rescuing heroes in our "helping" stories that we don't recognize when we've become the villains, sacrificing others' needs to meet our own.

Here are three ways we can take time to exhale and keep good help from going bad.

1. Distinguish helping from meddling

Some situations fall squarely in the "helping" category, such as these:

- advocating for those who cannot advocate for themselves
- parenting children based on their maturity level
- fulfilling predecided roles and division of labor

But in many areas of life, finding the line between helping and meddling is tricky business. I've spent much of my life swinging wildly between the two extremes, rushing in where I wasn't needed or withdrawing so completely that I abandoned people who actually needed me.

Helping	Meddling
by invitation	by invasion
asks and respects	assumes and presumes
meets another's needs	meets my needs (to control, feel important, etc.)
avoids needless, destructive pain and disappointment	prevents necessary pain and disappointment
moves people toward independence, growth, and maturity	makes people dependent, stunted, and entitled

When in doubt? OFFER to help. Let others know what you are willing and able to do. Then let them make the next move.

2. Keep an "I was wrong" list

(I know what you're thinking, but hear me out!)

Start a simple, *unemotional* list of things you thought you were right about, but it turns out you were not.

For example, on Facebook recently I made some predictions about what might happen during an upcoming episode of a favorite TV show. However, when I watched the episode, I discovered that none of what I predicted ended up happening.

Why did I add this to my "I was wrong" list?

Because when you only document when you're right, you start to believe that you're always right . . . or at least a lot righter than most people.

An "I was wrong" list will help keep pride in check, help humility grow, and help you think twice before assuming you always know what's best.

Because you have hard evidence that sometimes, you don't.

3. Practice NOT-ing

If you're a DOer, NOT-ing may well be the hardest thing you'll ever do.

NOT jumping in. NOT taking over. NOT correcting errors. NOT straightening things that are off-kilter. NOT fixing what's broken. NOT telling everyone the right way to get things done.

Recently, I was grumbling to a friend, "We don't even have a real verb in the English language for NOT-ing. *NOT-ing* isn't even a word. I want a real verb for what we ARE doing when we NOT!"

Later, it occurred to me that we do have a verb for NOT-ing. It's called TRUSTING.

Trusting that He is God . . . and we are NOT.

What Can Happen When a Problem Preventer Stops Meddling

While I was writing this chapter, I was involved with a frustrating work-related miscommunication. It wasn't the first time—or even the fifth time—this exact miscommunication had occurred.

Every other time, I had seen it coming, thrown on my heroic rescuer cape, and prevented the miscommunication from impacting anyone else. But this time, Rebekah's story was fresh in my mind and heart.

So I chose to NOT intervene. NOT fix. NOT meddle.

All that NOT-ing felt like I was *failing to help* my co-workers. Failing to help them made me feel like I was failing them . . . and causing the communication failure. The work-related miscommunication kerfuffle lasted about fifteen uncomfortable minutes during which a dozen or so people were mildly inconvenienced.

Then—without my help—a new process was quickly hammered out to prevent such miscommunications in the future.

I was stunned. *Why didn't they do this before?*

The answer was obvious: Each time I'd stepped in and meddled, I hadn't just prevented the immediate problem, I'd prevented its long-term solution.

If, like Amy and me, you're worn-out from all the hero missions you've been flying, here's a revolutionary idea:

What if our people don't need more heroes? What if they need more competent mistakes?

And what if the real hero isn't the woman who prevents problems . . . but the woman who lets necessary problems happen?

What might it feel like to stop swooping in to rescue?

To learn to NOT and truly trust that God is God, and we are not?

Go ahead. You can do it.

Take a deep breath.

And . . .

Exhale.

Now hang up your problem-preventer cape.

For good.

✳ *now breathe*

Spend a day documenting when you *unnecessarily*

___ jump in

___ take over

___ correct errors

___ straighten things out

___ fix things

___ tell people the right way to do things

___ prevent problems

___ other: _____

Pray-cess which ONE you will practice NOT-ing while you practice TRUSTING that God is God, and you are NOT.

And each time you NOT, be sure to go ahead and breathe that sigh of relief!

(You'll find a fun record-keeping sheet you can download and print at ExhaleBook.com!)

LOSE WHO YOU'RE NOT:

You're NOT *the fixer of every problem.*

seven

You're Not Alone: So Join the Women Flipping Their Flops

Amy

Oops. I did it again. My zealousness in a meeting led to words of fiery passion instead of gentle wisdom, and I was wallowing in the shame of failure. Those stupid sin patterns that keep me stuck. I want to be different. I really do, but some days I feel like a hopeless case. I seem to stick my foot in my mouth over and over again.

In my angst, I seriously started considering the tattoo again. As a woman who tends to overtalk, I've joked for years that I need Proverbs 10:19 (NLT) tattooed on my forehead: "Too much talk leads to sin. Be sensible and keep your mouth shut." Or maybe the placement should be on my hand where I can see it *before* I speak.

When I reached out to a friend in the same meeting, she told me that she, too, was feeling shameful because of something she had shared. Her issue was different, but our questions were the same. Maybe you're still wrestling with some of what we addressed in this first section, wondering what we wondered. Can we ever really change? Can we shed our sin, our faux pas, and our past to become the women we long to be? Will we ever be able to truly lose who we're not, letting go of those traits keeping us stuck, and shed who we don't want to be?

In chapter 1, I boldly proclaimed that change is possible, but after my meeting when my mouth torpedoed me *again*, I sank into doubt. My guess is that you wouldn't have picked up this book unless you felt part of our club of floppers, women stuck in an endless cycle of failures, overdeveloped responsibility, buying into labels of the past, living without boundaries, and fixing. We need to lose these things once and for all, but we need a path blazer, someone who shows us the way.

A Flopper's Mascot

Fortunately, Scripture records the stories of a flawed mascot who gives us great hope. His name is Peter. Oh, Peter. Passionate, impetuous Peter. (So much like a certain girl I know well!)

We know Peter for so many things—fishing, being one of Jesus's closest friends, walking on water—but the story that might most define him is the one we'd least want told about ourselves. Peter betrayed Jesus not once but three times. *Three times.* Let's pause, put ourselves in Peter's shoes for a moment, and feel the excruciating pain of that colossal failure.

How does he go from standing on a mountaintop, seeing the transformed Christ in all His glory, to denying that he even knew Jesus? I believe the answer is revealed the night *before* someone said, "This man was with him" (Luke 22:56). It's a huge insight into how we flop and how we can avoid flopping, so his story is worth a second look. Peter chooses the path to failure in one of the most intimate moments Jesus shared with His disciples around the table of the Last Supper. Here's the scene:

> Then Jesus told them, "This very night you will all fall away on account of me, for it is written: 'I will strike the shepherd, and the

sheep of the flock will be scattered.' But after I have risen, I will go ahead of you into Galilee."

Peter replied, "Even if all fall away on account of you, I never will."

"Truly I tell you," Jesus answered, "this very night, before the rooster crows, you will disown me three times."

But Peter declared, "Even if I have to die with you, I will never disown you." And all the other disciples said the same.

Matthew 26:31–35

Let's dissect each piece of this interaction to see where Peter starts down the road to his greatest shame.

Then Jesus told them, "This very night you will all fall away on account of me, for it is written: 'I will strike the shepherd, and the sheep of the flock will be scattered.' But after I have risen, I will go ahead of you into Galilee."

Jesus is so good! Not only does He quote Zechariah 13:7 here to give Peter and all posterity one more proof of His prophetic authenticity, but I also hear a warning softened with a promise. In Amy-style, Jesus might have said, "Hey, guys. This is going to be really hard, and you're not going to make it. But it's okay. Even though you're going to leave me, I'm not going to leave you."

Has God ever whispered to you a warning of an upcoming flop?

"If you take on that extra project, you're going to end up exhausted and overwhelmed."

"If you say yes to that unreasonable request, you're going to end up resenting her."

"If you volunteer for that position just because no one else has, you'll be working in your weakness, not your gifts."

"If you don't seek healing for that label someone slapped on you, you'll never believe you're enough."

I know our good God has given me those kinds of heads-up messages. Sometimes I've heeded them, but often, I've responded like Peter.

78

Peter replied, "Even if all fall away on account of you, I never will."

Gracious. Let's consider this answer. Peter argues with both the authority of an Old Testament prophet and the person of Jesus. It's a spectacular underestimate to call it a bold move, but Peter is determined.

It seems that Peter has come to see determination as his superpower. Do you hear any of yourself in these statements that I've used as I've blown past God's warnings with determination and self-sufficiency?

If I just keep a positive attitude . . .

If I just believe deeply enough . . .

If I just work hard enough . . .

At this point, I imagine Jesus taking a deep breath and trying again.

"Truly I tell you," Jesus answered, "this very night, before the rooster crows, you will disown me three times."

Once again Peter contradicts Jesus:

But Peter declared, "Even if I have to die with you, I will never disown you."

Peter's declaration seems so bold, so strong, and so true that all the other disciples join in defending themselves against Jesus. Can you imagine? Peter goes from personal revolt to leading a full-out mutiny.

Peter is loud. He is determined. He even influences others to follow him.

But he still fails. Peter denies Jesus just the way He predicted.

I've been there. Have you? Defending my schedule. Justifying my decisions. Arguing my points. Flexing determination and my ability to push through as though they're my superpowers.

All the while, the wide-awake nights are still happening. My joy is still leaking away. Close relationships are still suffering.

How do we lose who we're not—pseudo-superpowers included—once and for all? Peter shows us how failure patterns start, but he shows us the way out, too.

The Look on Jesus's Face

It's a sad story. Peter does exactly what Jesus warned; he denies Jesus three times. Peter flops spectacularly.

First, he folds when a girl recognizes him (Matthew 26:69–70).

Then he denies Jesus with an oath (v. 72).

Finally, he calls down curses on himself before exclaiming that he doesn't know Jesus (v. 74).

The more he entrenches himself in his lie, the deeper the shame hole gets, and then the thing that he probably dreaded most happens. Peter knows that Jesus knows.

In Luke's account of the story, he describes it like this:

> Peter replied, "Man, I don't know what you're talking about!" Just as he was speaking, the rooster crowed. The Lord turned and looked straight at Peter. Then Peter remembered the word the Lord had spoken to him: "Before the rooster crows today, you will disown me three times." And he went outside and wept bitterly.
>
> Luke 22:60–62

Oh, the heartbreak! Jesus knows. He was right about Peter, and He's right about us. It's not about trying harder. Determination and bold declarations don't cut it. We don't need a superpower. We need a Savior.

But in that moment, Peter must have thought he had lost his Savior in his denials. I've felt the same when I've ignored God, gone my own way, and suffered the consequences. I've thought that His disappointment in me would leave me on my own to change.

As I studied the Luke story, I started wondering about Jesus's face when He looked at Peter. I know how I'd look if someone treated me the way Peter had treated Jesus. The look on my face would be disappointment. Or disgust. It might be a look of hurt or betrayal.

Thankfully, Jesus isn't like me. Because He always had to be true to His own character, we know the look on Jesus's face as He looked at Peter. He gazed at Peter with love. With compassion and mercy. His look was one of grace.

How Jesus Looks at Us

When we know we need to change, we truly do need a mindset reset. As I said back in chapter 1, we need to shift from a fixed mindset to a growth mindset, but why?

Because embedded in the growth mindset is the concept of grace. You're not a disappointment to God or a hopeless case. Knowing that you're not perfect but constantly growing is the biggest exhale ever.

However, finding grace is a tricky thing. It requires more than just being determined to change our mind. We can give ourselves some grace, but it's limited. Only our Savior's grace is limitless.

Jesus looked at Peter with love and grace when Peter was at his lowest point, the moment of his greatest failure. Jesus looks at you and me with love and grace when we're at our weakest, most exhausted state. He sees our flops—every single one—that have led to our depleted life and reduced sense of self. He knows them fully while fully reaching out to us with the boundless grace we need to escape the life we've created. The grace we need to change and to lose who we're not. We can look back to Peter's situation to find two ways to flip our flops.

The Redemptive Flip

One of my favorite passages in all of Scripture is found in the last chapter of John, where he records the redemption story of Peter's denials. To summarize quickly,

Peter abandons Jesus.
> Peter denies Jesus.
>> Jesus is crucified.
>>> Jesus is resurrected.
>>>> Peter goes fishing.

The Sea of Galilee on which his boat bobs is filled with memories of Jesus, and Peter has to be thinking of them. . . .

When Jesus stilled the wind and the waves there. When He provided the tax in the fish's mouth from these very waters. When He fed the multitudes as they sat on the banks. And certainly the day when Jesus called Peter to following instead of fishing.

How sweet these memories must be to Peter, and how bitter the residual taste of his betrayals.

Suddenly, Peter sees a man on the shore. John knows Him first, but Peter acts first. (Oh, beautiful, impetuous Peter.) It's Jesus!

Peter *flings* himself out of the boat toward Jesus. In that moment, and then in an exquisite interaction of grace found in John 21, Peter turns away from his denials back into the love and grace of Jesus. In short, Peter repents.

That's where we need to start, too. Need to lose who you're not? Need to turn away from all the flops? Need more grace than you can muster up to face the difficulties of a shift? That's what repentance is for, and that's what our Savior is here to do. When we need deep change, we repent, receive grace, and start fresh.

Peter's glorious postflop story should encourage us. Weeks after this meeting with Jesus, Peter is no longer denying but boldly proclaiming that "God has made this Jesus, whom you crucified, both Lord and Messiah" (Acts 2:36) in front of a huge crowd. Talk about a stunning Holy Spirit–powered change!

The Preemptive Flip

Repentance is the first step toward change if we've already experienced the failure, but is there any hope for opting out of the school of hard knocks? I'm convinced there is.

When Jesus first told Peter that all the disciples would leave Him, Peter could have responded differently. Instead of being determined and defensive, Peter could have been humble. He could have recognized his own weakness and flaws. Instead of arguing with Jesus, he could have cried out to Him, asking for the strength and grace that he needed to walk through the coming days.

Jesus's isolation was foretold by a prophet, so I believe that the disciples' abandonment was set in the divine time line. I wondered, though, was Peter's denial prophesied? I searched and searched the Old Testament, finding nothing about a disciple's denial, and then I asked some scholarly friends. They also could find no prediction about Peter's failure.

That leads me to believe that if Peter's reactions to Jesus had been different, his story could have been different.

Let's lose who we're not and then stay out of the weeds. When God whispers the warning about our decisions and commitments, let's listen and obey. When He shows us our weaknesses, let's humbly plead for His strength to rush into our gaps. When Jesus speaks from His Word, let's break out our highlighters and learn. This is the preemptive flip, the one that happens *before* our flop. If we react to God's warnings by turning to Him for the help we can't live without, many times we can avoid the pain of failure completely.

Leveraging the Pain

You probably bought this book and started reading because you were already in pain. The pain of the pressure that's on you. The pain of trying to fulfill so many expectations. The pain of missing the life you know you're made to live. Can I give you a weird invitation? I invite you to lean into the pain. It's not a fun part of the process, but it's a necessary first step. We can even be thankful for it. Our pain points to our problem.

Peter's pain made him ready to fling himself out of the boat toward Jesus. Peter's pain propelled him toward The Ultimate Solution, Jesus himself, standing on the shore.

Let's do the same. Flinging ourselves toward Him. Trusting that His love and grace alone create the change we need. We simply pay attention to the pain, seek Him for solutions, and join our energies to His work in us.

Change is possible. Lose who you're not. This is a giant first step.

❋ now breathe

In a quiet time and space, fling your heart toward Jesus. Repent and ask for forgiveness where your self-sufficiency requires it. Then humbly ask Jesus to create change in your weakness with His astounding power. Ask Him to help you lose who you're not once and for all.

LOSE WHO YOU'RE NOT:

You're NOT *a hopeless case.*

Part One Quick Reference Guide to
Lose Who You're NOT

You're NOT permanently stuck.
You're NOT required to be perfect.
You're NOT responsible for everyone all the time.
You're NOT defined by old labels.
You're NOT boundaryless.
You're NOT the fixer of every problem.
You're NOT a hopeless case.

Old Mindset . . .	*New Mindset . . .*
It's too late for me to change.	Jesus creates empowered change.
My failures are the worst thing in the world.	God uses my failures to help me grow.
I'm responsible for all that people expect of me.	The Holy Spirit guides me to fulfill legitimate needs.
I am a girl gripped by fear.	I am a woman held by faith.
Setting boundaries means I'm selfish.	Knowing my Father's business helps me set clear boundaries.
I must fix anything that's broken.	God calls me to help, not meddle.
I'm a disappointment to God.	Jesus loves me and stands ready to flip my flops.

Part Two

LOVE WHO YOU ARE

When we're nervous, one side effect of a fear-induced adrenaline rush is breathlessness.

Being breathless isn't good for girls hiking a pathway toward change. Not at all. If we don't address it, everything shakes—our knees, our hands, and especially our voices—forestalling our ability to move forward.

One simple solution is square breathing. Here's how you do it in four easy steps:

1. Exhale slowly through your mouth, counting to four as you do.
2. Hold for four even counts.
3. Inhale slowly through your nose for four counts.
4. Hold for four counts, then repeat.

In the first section of the book, we asked you to exhale, ridding yourself of the pressures that have kept you from living the life God has for you, the life you long for.

In this section, we want you to inhale. Take it all in!

Breathe deep and gaze with intent at the new scenery around you as you travel.

Explore, identify, and enjoy the gifts God gave you and the very fiber with which He made you.

Embrace the truth of who God created you to be.

In losing who you're NOT, you realized that you're *less* than you've tried to be.

Now it's time to inhale, loving who you ARE and understanding that God made you *more* than you've ever known.

Let God fill you with hope and joy in this new phase of your journey!

eight

Love Your Uniqueness: Because There's Only One You

Cheri

"Well, goody, goody gumdrops for you!"

I should be sleeping; instead, I'm talking back to the guy in the antibullying video I'm watching on Facebook.

He's just explained the best way to render a bully powerless is "just don't *react*." Which probably makes sense to a lot of people. But for me, the little word "just" is like dropping a lighted match on dry pine needles.

"HELLO—I'm so glad it's easy for you, but it's so hard for some of us who are easily triggered!"

It's 9:55 p.m., and I am supposed to be asleep by 10:00. I switch my cell phone to airplane mode, set it on my nightstand, and close my eyes.

But "just don't react" has gotten under my skin.

I'm mad at that guy.

Mostly, though, I'm mad at myself.

I should have "just don't react" figured out by now. But I don't.

Which means that many people who do not matter have had too much authority over my life. They've had authority about my identity, my worth, my actions, my inactions.

I remember the difference between *expert* and *authority* from a class I'm taking: An expert is someone who knows a lot, while an authority is someone we actually listen to.

This further deepens my concern over giving the wrong people so much authority in my life. I have listened to far too many people who didn't even know me.

I reach for my phone, switch it off airplane mode, and text myself:

I have let people take authority over me. I am learning boundaries that allow me to choose whom to give authority. I can say, "Your voice doesn't matter, and you have no authority in my life. You may speak, I can hear, but I don't have to listen, and I don't have to internalize. And I don't have to authorize your words."

I turn my phone off, set it back on the nightstand, and pray as I drift off to sleep: "Okay, Lord, this feels big. REALLY big. But what on earth does it look like in real life?"

He answers. Big time. I wake up to this burning question: *How do I un-authorize someone?* And immediately I think: *Un-authorize is a totally lame word.*

I try to come up with a word that means "take authority away from someone." There's *unauthorized*, but that's passive and past tense. I want a word that means that regardless of how someone has come to have authority in my life—whether the person took authority from me or I gave authority to that person—I am now rescinding it.

The next thirty minutes remind me of how excruciating the English language can be, as I go to Thesaurus.com, look at all the synonyms for *authorize*, and try to think of their "un-" version.

Nuthin'.

I'm no longer simply curious; I'm now on the verge of desperation. I need an active verb that means removing someone's authority in my life and over my life.

So I go back through the list of synonyms for *authorize* again, just in case I missed something the first time.

Nope. . . . Nope. . . . Nope. . . . Wait!

appoint

Another word for *authorize* is *appoint*.

Yes.

But do we have an "un-" version for *appoint*?

Prickles of recognition tap-dance across my scalp.

Do we ever.

It's a word I've been working myself to death to avoid for my entire life:

dis-appoint

The key to "just don't react" is dis-appointing people.

The very thing we try so hard not to do. Haven't we spent our lives trying to please our people? Be who they want us to be? Do what they need us to do?

Yet dis-appointing people is the very thing we need to do.

What Dis-Appointing People Looks Like in Action

When I initially shared this concept of dis-appointing people with Amy during a *Grit 'n' Grace* convo, she was dumbstruck. After the episode aired, we received a flood of comments and emails from listeners all saying, "This concept is a game changer. But what does dis-appointing people look like in real life?"

In John 9:1–38, we can observe a man dis-appointing people in various positions of authority: his neighbors and townspeople, the Pharisees, even his own parents!

His story starts at a place we're all familiar with: the location of blame.

Jesus's disciples ask, "Rabbi, who sinned, this man or his parents, that he was born blind?"

In other words, "Whose fault is this?" The question that turns us into quivering bowls of Jell-O. Because when others hold authority over us, we're reduced to just one plea: *Please don't pin the blame on me.*

Follow this man's interactions with others once his sight has been restored.

When people who knew him as The Man Born Blind ask him, "How then were your eyes opened?" he says, "The man they call Jesus made some mud and put it on my eyes. He told me to go to Siloam and wash. So I went and washed, and then I could see."

In the New International Version, this is a thirty-three-word answer; watch how this number changes.

The Man Born Blind is taken to the Pharisees, who also ask how he's received his sight. Notice what happens to his answer: "He put mud on my eyes . . . and I washed, and now I see." His story is down to thirteen words, and it's about to get even shorter still.

The arrogant authorities . . . er . . . Pharisees argue among themselves about Jesus because He made mud on the Sabbath.

That's right.

Instead of celebrating that this man born blind NOW CAN SEE, they're fussing about a man-made rule. Instead of believing the man's testimony about his own experience, the Pharisees call in his parents.

It's such a sad moment. Their responses tell us so much about the power arrogant authorities hold over us and the joy they deny us. Shouldn't this be the happiest day of those parents' lives? Isn't this what they prayed for in the days and weeks after their son was born? Isn't this the answer to the prayer they quit praying years ago, when the discouragement and shame became too much?

Isn't this proof that they can stop praying silent prayers of desperation—*Please don't pin the blame on me*—because their son's blindness was never about their sin after all? Shouldn't they be celebrating that their son now can see and that their own hearts are now set free?

But the parents are scared of the bullies, and they haven't seen the "just don't react" Facebook video. They try to appease the Pharisees, who dismiss them, call back their son, and ask him to tell his story again.

They need him to alter his story so they come out looking good—which is what arrogant authorities always need from us.

As they prompt him, "Give glory to God by telling the truth. . . . We know this man [Jesus] is a sinner," their subtext is crystal clear.

You know what this is like; you've been in this exact same place, too.

"Your story can't possibly be true."

"Tell a new version."

"Say what we want to hear."

"Don't you dare disappoint us."

You're surrounded by arrogant authorities—or perhaps you're face-to-face with one powerful arrogant authority—and you're reduced to just one plea: *Please don't pin the blame on me.*

And you're ready to say whatever it takes to keep from disappointing them. To avoid disapproval. Because disapproval equals death. You start to open your mouth to babble the usual torrent of ingratiations and explanations and conciliations and equivocations and . . .

Wait. What is this man saying?

"Whether he is a sinner or not, I don't know."

Uh-oh. He's disagreeing with them. They're not going to like this. At. All.

"One thing I do know."

One thing? I was about to spend the next twenty minutes apologizing for all sorts of things. How does he distill it down to one thing?

"I was blind but now I see."

From thirty-three to thirteen to seven words.

I was blind but now I see.

The truth in its simplest form.

He knows it because it happened to him. They may not like it, but they can't take it from him. He is the authority on his own experience with Jesus.

If you want to know what dis-appointing others looks like in real life, listen and learn from his unflinching willingness to tell the truth.

When the Pharisees ask, "What did he do to you? How did he open your eyes?" he responds, "I have told you already and you did not listen. Why do you want to hear it again? Do you want to become his disciples too?"

Talk about gutsy!

The argument escalates as the Pharisees try to pin the blame on him. But they don't matter to him because he has already dis-appointed them. They have no authority over him now that he's experienced Jesus. After all, because of Jesus he NOW CAN SEE.

Put yourself in his place. The Pharisees send you away yet again. Having lived in darkness since birth, you're marveling at all you can see around you for the very first time in your entire life.

And you're on a mission: trying to find the One who has given you this extravagant gift of sight so you can thank Him. You were still blind when He told you to go wash off the mud He'd put on your eyes, so you don't know what He looks like.

As you're searching, someone taps you on the shoulder. You turn around and sense that He's been looking for you . . . and that you know Him from somewhere.

"Do you believe in the Son of Man?" He asks.

He knows Jesus? Great! He can help you in your quest.

"Who is he, sir?" you ask. "Tell me so that I may believe in him."

He responds, "You have now seen him; in fact, he is the one speaking with you."

Of course—His voice! You recognize His voice!

And with your next words and deeds, you recognize Jesus—"the light of the world" who has brought light to your world—as the one and only Righteous Authority in your life.

"Lord, I believe," you say. And you worship Him.

Two Steps to Dis-Appointing Others

If you've been stumbling in the darkness of attempting to please and appease people for your entire life, you're not alone.

But here's the good news: You don't have to stay stuck in darkness.

Living in the light of the One who restores your sight leads you to dis-appoint everyone else.

You practice a new response to others' faultfinding.

Go ahead and try to pin the blame on me. It won't stick, because I've already dis-appointed you.

When your confidence in your newfound 20/20 vision makes them say, "How dare you lecture us!" you remember seven simple words: *I was blind but now I see.*

And as often as necessary, you dis-appoint people by reliving the moment you met Jesus: "Lord, I believe," you say (step 1); and you worship Him (step 2).

Learning to Live within Our Limits

Why so much talk about dis-appointing?

Because we've tried to be "all things to all people" for far too long.

Which, by the way, is a phrase that does come from Scripture. But the way we apply it, by stretching ourselves far beyond our limits, is often far from biblical.

A young woman who had recently sustained a permanent back injury once told me, "I'm learning to live within my limits. Even though I'm doing less, I feel more free." It made me wonder, *Why does it take an injury or illness for us to recognize that we have limits?*

Now, I know from experience that if you tell a group of women that they have "limits," they'll react as if you've slapped them in the face. We'd rather kill ourselves trying to prove that we can "do it all" than accept the truth:

You. Have. Limits.

The only One who has none goes by the name God.

Embrace your limits. Merely recognizing and accepting them isn't enough. In order to love who you ARE, you've got to narrow your focus to who you truly are. Which excludes who you wish you were and who others think you should be.

Sounds crazy, and certainly countercultural, I know. But what if God actually means what He says in Ephesians 2:10—that you are His unique masterpiece, created to do the good things He planned for you long ago?

What if—instead of being all things to all people—you're meant to specialize? What if you are a limited edition of one? What if limits actually set you free—free to lose who you're NOT and love who you ARE?

Free to focus on your one-of-a-kind specialty?

Loving Your Limits

If you're like Amy and me, you have a lifelong habit that gets in the way of learning to dis-appoint other people and embrace your limits.

It's the habit of overapologizing—saying "I'm sorry!" for things that don't need an apology, while failing to seek forgiveness for those that do.

To identify and break this hardwired habit, take the No Faux-pologies Challenge. Here's how it works:

DO apologize

- when you are wrong.
- when you are right . . . the wrong way.
- when you hurt someone.
- when the Holy Spirit convicts you to seek forgiveness for sin.

But—and this is vital—just because you feel bad about a situation doesn't automatically mean that the Holy Spirit is convicting you. Not all of the guilt you feel is yours to feel.

You don't need to apologize when someone

- disagrees with you.
- dislikes you.

- feels inconvenienced. (Especially if they're whining. Apologizing to a whiner just cranks up their volume and frequency!)

Most importantly, stop apologizing for being your authentic self. Which may include (for starters):

- being tired
- having emotions
- getting sick
- succeeding
- having different personal preferences
- saying a necessary no
- snorting when you laugh
- holding unique beliefs and opinions
- making an honest mistake
- being bumped into by someone else
- asking questions
- taking up space in this world
- desiring change

Why does this matter?

Because Jesus is the one true Authority in your life. What He calls you to do rarely pleases arrogant authorities.

Practice dis-appointing anyone who has too much authority in your life by reminding yourself throughout each day: *I am uniquely and wonderfully created by God. I'm embracing who I am—with no faux-pologies!*

 *now breathe*

Make a list of the things you apologize for and keep track for the next seven to ten days—or until you see distinctive repeating patterns.

Pray-cess which true apologies should stay . . . and which faux-pologies should go.

(You'll find a fun record-keeping sheet you can download and print at ExhaleBook.com!)

LOVE WHO YOU ARE:

You ARE a limited edition of one.

nine

Love Your Creator:
Because Your Whole Story Has Purpose

Amy

Our *Grit 'n' Grace* podcast listeners frequently share with us their hurts and struggles. When I read these emails, I always tear up, not only because I feel sad for these women, but because I've felt the same way. Here are a couple of email excerpts to show you what I mean:

> If there is one person that hates me and 99 that love me, I will forget the 99 and go after the one . . . practically obsessing over what could be wrong with me to make a person dislike me. It's exhausting!

> My biggest struggle with people-pleasing and perfectionism is wanting to be loved, accepted, and included. It's all based on those needs/desires that get me overcommitted, burned-out, and doing things I don't want to do.

Do you identify, too? So many of us feel it's selfish or unattainable to know our strengths and love our authentic self.

We can start to feel disqualified for God's fullest life for lots of reasons. Often, it's because of the things that are entirely outside our control. It might be the color of your skin or your nationality. It might be a health issue, a loss you've suffered, or a tragedy you've faced. It could be that you weren't loved well as a child or that you were abandoned by someone who claimed to love you. Hard circumstances can make us feel that our story is stacked against us.

My heart screeched to a shattering stop one day when my friend Debbie said it this way: "Women spend the first half of their lives not living fully because they don't think they're enough—not old enough, not experienced enough, not skillful enough. Women spend the second half of their lives not living fully because they think they're too much—too old, too irrelevant, too out-of-touch."

I cringed because I know what Debbie said is true of so many. But I don't want to be one of those women, those who have missed their entire life because they believed they fell short—that their story disqualified them. I'll bet you don't want to miss out, either.

How do we shrug off the pattern Debbie described, learning to love all of who we are and our whole story? Just as in square breathing, you go through intentional cycles of exhaling and inhaling. Exhale the lies you've believed . . . two, three, four. Inhale God's truth about you . . . two, three, four. Exhale the labels you've worn . . . two, three, four. Inhale God's gifts in you . . . two, three, four. Exhale your need to please others . . . two, three, four. Inhale God's love for you . . . two, three, four. Exhale and inhale over and over again until the shaking subsides, your heart stops racing, and you step into your truest God-created self—the woman who made God smile when He dreamed you up.

Just Breathe

We need a leader to take us by the hand, showing us how to take intentional breaths that help us see our story in a new light. We find that leader in Scripture. There's a woman, a woman with a tough backstory, who had an encounter with Jesus that gives us a glimpse into how rethinking our personal history can help us love who we are. We don't know her name, but she's known in the Bible simply as a Canaanite woman. Hold on to your hat. This passage is tough, but we'll unpack it together.

> Leaving that place, Jesus withdrew to the region of Tyre and Sidon. A Canaanite woman from that vicinity came to him, crying out, "Lord, Son of David, have mercy on me! My daughter is demon-possessed and suffering terribly."
>
> Jesus did not answer a word. So his disciples came to him and urged him, "Send her away, for she keeps crying out after us."
>
> He answered, "I was sent only to the lost sheep of Israel."
>
> The woman came and knelt before him. "Lord, help me!" she said.
>
> He replied, "It is not right to take the children's bread and toss it to the dogs."
>
> "Yes it is, Lord," she said. "Even the dogs eat the crumbs that fall from their master's table."
>
> Then Jesus said to her, "Woman, you have great faith! Your request is granted." And her daughter was healed at that moment.
>
> Matthew 15:21–28

Although this passage is puzzling, there are some golden nuggets here for those of us who find it hard to love the story we're living.

External Divides Aren't a Reason to Despair or Compare

For the Canaanite woman, there were two external factors, parts of her story outside of her control, that should have separated her from Jesus. Instead, they brought her near. She was a Canaanite, a Gentile, which automatically made her an outsider to the Jewish nation, commissioned by God to be separate. According to Jewish laws and traditions, Jesus had no business with any Canaanite woman.

But she had a second trait that made her "other." She was also the mother of a demon-possessed child. As sisters who understand struggle, let's ponder that for a moment. We may not be able to imagine exactly what parenting a demon-possessed child was like, but we all know the pain of being outside the norm. The whispers of judgment must have created self-doubt and pain for our Canaanite friend. She and her child weren't invited to any play groups. Her baby probably played alone on the playground. Being a parental pariah, loaded on top of the agony of having a suffering child, made for one hurting heart.

But the pain points of these external divides were the very things that drew her close to Jesus. She didn't let her identity align with the people around her, limiting her options. She aligned her identity with the limitless One, crying out to Him with tremendous pain but bigger hope. She didn't sink into self-pity. Instead, she rose to the occasion.

Her words reveal her heart as she calls him "Lord" and "Son of David," signs that she believed in Him as God and Messiah. Her need of Jesus's healing power pulled her irresistibly toward Him. Breaking the traditions of the pagan people around her who followed powerless idols, she fixed her eyes on Jesus as the source of her help. She had nowhere else to turn, so she turned to just the right person.

Do you have difficult circumstances that make you feel automatically disqualified? What if you changed the way you thought about them, like the Canaanite woman did? We can look at our flaws, failures, and external limits as factors that make us strangely different or an outsider, things that keep us from our fullest life. Or we can start to see those same traits as things that draw us to Jesus, and we can become grateful for the way they make us dependent on Him. Gratitude transforms our flaws into fortitude. The Canaanite woman didn't give up because she was a Gentile with a demon-possessed child. She leveraged those needs to stoke her determination to get to Jesus. Instead of keeping her from Him, her barriers built her faith.

Loving ourselves—every piece of our story, not just the easy parts—is part of loving our Creator. Our difficulties also make us glorious! If we don't accept our God-given narrative, our story is left tragically unshared, and the world is left with a hole that we were meant to fill.

Times of Testing Are Training

Not only does our Canaanite friend show us how to see our differences and difficulties in a whole new way, she blazes a hope-filled trail, displaying how to deal with disappointments and confusing circumstances.

I haven't heard this challenging passage taught much, and I totally resisted when I felt God nudge me to use it for this chapter. Let's just be honest. Verses 23–27 make us wonder about Jesus. When our Canaanite friend cries out for help, Jesus responds, "It is not right to take the children's bread and toss it to the dogs." How could He say such a harsh thing to a hurting woman who sought Him out? We don't want to talk about it because it's confusing.

To unravel it all, I reminded myself of the Principle of Intention, Jesus's pray-cessed purpose in everything He said and did. When I thought about that principle, in addition to some truths from the Old Testament, His seemingly cruel words to this woman began to lose their sting. They stopped seeming like a contradiction to who we believe Jesus is, kind and merciful, and affirmed the goodness of His divine character.

Think back to three of our Old Testament friends. God tested Abraham by asking him to sacrifice his son Isaac, but in the end, God gave a ram as a way out (Genesis 22). Jacob wrestled with God, and he walked away with both a limp and a nation (Genesis 32). Job was tested, too, and he gives us a glimpse of the purpose behind it when he says, "But he knows the way that I take; when he has tested me, I will come forth as gold" (Job 23:10).

In Jesus's confusing response to the Canaanite woman, we can stand on these truths:

- God is always the same, never changing; testing is one way He teaches and strengthens His people.
- Jesus, His Son, intentionally said and did only what His Father told Him.

Jesus tested the Canaanite woman's faith with His words, and it came out shining brightly. His seemingly heartless words brought good into the situation, not hurt. Commentators support this final analysis.

Faith, her greatest gift, was created in her by God and then called out by His Son. Jesus's exclamation, "Woman, you have great faith!" wasn't just personal praise for her heart but a statement to the people watching. Here He was declaring His love and acceptance of Gentiles. On this occasion, His first foray outside of Israel, Jesus had an interaction with a Gentile woman that was recorded for us to read thousands of years later. An accident? Not at all. It was a holy statement, and a Gentile woman got the gift of being part of it.

You may have picked up this book because you were weary. Because you had gotten off track. Because you couldn't find your way back to the life that you were created to live. Because the external circumstances of your story seem like ones you can't overcome. Life's been painful, but it doesn't have to be purposeless.

We can embrace our difficult story as part of His work in us. God uses times of testing to train us. Jesus's questioning didn't destroy the Canaanite woman's faith. It strengthened it, and then the reward came.

Jesus Gives a Feast, Not Crumbs

After enduring silence, a rebuke, and a seemingly harsh reply from Jesus, the Canaanite woman responded, "Even the dogs eat the crumbs that fall from their master's table."

What a quick response and a tremendous statement of faith!

She was saying, "Even your crumbs would be enough for me." It makes me tear up just to type it. She was still so hope-filled and undeterred. She steadfastly believed in Him.

But what about us? Do we believe that Jesus's crumbs are enough to redeem our story? To qualify us for His bigger story? Or in our heart of hearts, do we believe He's holding the good stuff back for others while we get nothing but the leftovers?

Years ago, I was doing a word study of the Greek word *agape*, typically defined as God's unconditional and lavish love. But it was another definition that stopped me in my tracks. As I read the analysis of the original biblical language, "a feast" caught my eye. That flash of insight flattened me. God gives us His love as a feast, and Jesus proved it in this story. He didn't just pat the woman on the head with a compliment. He didn't partially fulfill her request to heal her daughter. The passage says that her daughter was *"healed from that very hour"* (NKJV). Completely well! Not crumbs but the whole loaf of bread. A love feast.

Jesus is no miser. He's extravagant. He's lavish. Jesus is a feast-thrower, not a crumb-doler. I believe the Canaanite woman's quick response filled Jesus with delight and that He broke out in a wide smile as He proclaimed, "Woman, you have great faith! Your request is granted."

Through her weakness and need, Jesus had drawn her to himself. She had endured the test that showed her faith strong, and He *loved* it. Surely this woman He created must have basked in His praise and rewards.

Her difficult circumstances didn't disqualify her at all. In fact, her challenges strengthened her faith, and now her impact is eternal. Every single part of her life, especially the ones that seemed like disqualifiers, led to her defining moment with Jesus. Can you imagine how she'd love knowing that her story is part of His and that we're studying it today?

A Modern-Day Canaanite Woman

Jackie and Rebekah, identical twins, were two of my childhood friends that I lost touch with in college. Several years ago, through the miracle of Facebook, I reconnected with Jackie during a painful time in her life. In 2013, she was diagnosed with a rare form of stage four cancer that affected her facial structure and a brain nerve. In a matter of months, her marriage ended, she received the devastating diagnosis, and she was unemployed, unable to start a new job because of her upcoming surgeries.

But just as Jesus traveled to meet the Canaanite woman in the middle of her crisis, He met Jackie as she headed home after a meeting with doctors about treatment. She had been thinking about her dire circumstances and listening to the radio, but something told her to turn off the noise and sit in silence. As the car and her spirit quieted, she cried out to God, "How am I going to do this?"

God answered clearly, "You can do this because you have me, and you are loved."

"But how?" Jackie asked again.

"Because I will never leave you," God answered, and then He grew silent.

But peace filled the car, and Jackie knew that she had just experienced the tangible presence of God. In the midst of the worst turn of her life, a time when she felt she had gone from having everything to losing it all, God came to where Jackie was and spoke tenderly.

Just like the Canaanite woman, Jackie responded to her challenges with an undaunted faith, even on days filled with suffering. The surgeries and radiation that she went through to save her life have left her face scarred, her vision impaired, her hearing damaged, and her body in constant pain.

Instead of using my own words, I want you to hear Jackie's as she recorded them for family and friends on her CaringBridge site. This fight against cancer has been nothing less than horrific, but see if you can find the common redemptive thread. Here's Jackie. . . .

Feb. 15, 2013 (8 days before surgery)

Someone asked me why I have not gotten angry. How I'm not upset. But I look around me and I think, how can I be angry? My blessings are shown to me every day. Yes, I cry. I cry hard. It catches me by surprise and takes hold. But within moments I am able to gather myself and I see. I see around me. My child, by the grace of God, is healthy and happy. I am safe. I have family who loves and supports me. What a blessing! For some have none.

Feb. 22, 2013 (the day of Jackie's first surgery)

I pray that the things that need to get better will do so through this process. I pray for strength, courage, and endurance. I pray mostly for those who are also going through their own battles— over health, emotions, or situations. That He would touch them and help them through. For He is helping me. And all of you are helping me through this. Without you I would be handling this much differently.

March 5, 2013

I didn't think my appearance would really bother me that much. But honestly, it does. So that is why I have asked for those who haven't seen me not to stop by for now. Just the whole "package" is difficult for me . . . looks, eating, talking. It's a very different perspective that I will always remember. It's another blessing God has given me. For though we all think we know how those with handicaps feel, we really don't until we go through it. My lesson in humility.

Feb. 22, 2014 (a year post-surgery)

So many of you tell me that my words inspire others. My outlook is positive. Well, you know, not all of the time. But I do get there. Out of the things that frustrate me or hurt me, this is how I find the blessing. In everything difficult, painful and sad; there is a blessing in each and every one.

Y'all, I cannot tell you how difficult it was to shrink Jackie's big story into this small space. These journal samplings are just a glimpse of page after page of praise to God and an accounting of her blessings. In pain that most of us can't imagine . . . in confronting the reality that her face would never look like her twin's again . . . in managing co-parenting challenges . . . in it *all*, Jackie let gratitude write her story.

And gratitude transformed her pain into fortitude.

Just as Jesus sought out the Canaanite woman, He sought out Jackie before her crisis. Just as Jesus spoke words of praise over the Canaanite woman's faith, He spoke words of assurance over Jackie and built her faith through suffering. Just as the Canaanite's daughter was healed, so my friend Jackie has lived to proclaim her story, the story God has given her. A story told with overwhelming gratitude. She doesn't deny the hard parts, yet she focuses on the blessings. Jackie sees her life as a feast given by God, and her praise is infectious to all who hear her tell it.

Taking My Own Advice

I want my life to be infectious too, don't you? Here's a simple script that I've been using to shift my thinking. Instead of constantly saying, "I wish I were _____," focusing on the parts of my life that are different than I'd wish, I replace that sentence with "I'm thankful I'm _____."

Instead of saying, "I wish I were a Jew," maybe the Canaanite woman would have said, "I'm thankful God gave me the faith to believe."

Instead of saying, "I wish I didn't have cancer," Jackie has said, "I'm thankful I got to see my daughter graduate from elementary school."

I can fill in my blanks, too. Instead of saying things like, "I wish I hadn't experienced a broken heart years ago," I can say, "I'm thankful God has given me compassion for the brokenhearted."

Now you try. Fill in your blanks. Instead of "I wish I was _____," I'll now say, "I'm thankful for _____."

Reconnecting with Jackie, hearing her story, and experiencing her gratitude have changed me. Seeing how she has allowed God to shape her story through gratitude has made me determined to do the same through embracing the new script above and by doing some of that good ol' square breathing.

So here I go. . . .

"My mouth always gets me in trouble. . . ." Exhale . . . two, three, four.

"God created and uses my love of words. . . ." Inhale . . . two, three, four.

"Being a woman limits my opportunities. . . ." Exhale . . . two, three, four.

"God handmade me female for His unique purposes. . . ." Inhale . . . two, three, four.

"I worry that others will reject me. . . ." Exhale . . . two, three, four.

"Jesus accepts me and loves me more than I can imagine. . . ." Inhale . . . two, three, four. . . . Sigh.

☀ *now breathe*

Write down three ways God displays His creative power through you. It could be a difficulty that He uses to draw others to himself, a gift that He's given you, or a trial that He's purposed to strengthen your faith. Thank Him for loving you lavishly in these ways.

LOVE WHO YOU ARE:

You ARE a woman with a story linked to His.

Ten

Love Your Personality:
Because You're at Your Best as YOU

Cheri

When you look back into your childhood or teen years, who were the women whose lives positively influenced yours? The women who made you think to yourself—consciously or unconsciously—*When I grow up, I want to be just like her.*

My *her* was Florence Littauer.

When I was a preteen, my mother came home from a seminar and passed out personality quizzes to my father, my brother, and me. Once we'd tallied our results, her worst fears were confirmed: She was the only sane human being in a house full of crazy people!

The next day, she took me with her to the seminar, and I sat spellbound as Florence taught on the four personality types.

Florence gave me two things that day.

First, she gave me hope. Hope that my natural wiring wasn't wrong or bad just because it was different from my mother's. In fact, now that I think about it from the dis-appointing lens, she gave me my first dose of hope that I could disappoint my mother and still respect and love her by being exactly who God created me to be, even if that wasn't the image she had in her mind for me.

Second, Florence gave me a role model. Someone I could look at and think, *When I grow up, I want to be just like her.*

By *just like her* I actually meant one specific thing: I wanted to make people laugh the way Florence Littauer did. Unfortunately, I'm not funny. In fact, humor is one of my weaknesses. Yet for decades, I did the worst thing a not funny person can do: I tried really hard to become funnier.

The Sincerest Form of Flattery

At Leverage: The Speaker Conference, where Amy and I serve as mentors, aspiring speakers often confidently tell us, "My communication style is _____!" But when we hear them speak, what we see and hear in them is totally different from what they've told us.

Why the difference? For many, it's that early role model, the one who evoked *When I grow up, I want to be just like her.* They long to be like the women they have admired and appreciated—the women who have had such influence in their own lives.

They want to make that kind of difference. So they try really hard to become _____-er. Happier. Holier. Bolder. Braver. *Funnier.*

We've all tried to shore up our weaknesses and become _____-er. And while it's admirable to appreciate a mentor, there's a danger to trying to overcome our weaknesses in order to be *just like her.* The shift into sin is so subtle, we won't see it if we're not looking for it. Here's how it happens.

First, we recognize and appreciate the woman who's had a positive influence in our life. Next, we admire her and long to make this same difference in the lives of others. (So far, so good.)

Then—and herein lies the danger—we start to see this woman as our *ideal.* We focus on a few specific personality strengths she has that we don't. And we become driven to work on our weaknesses, certain that if we try hard enough we will become _____-er, *just like her*. But instead, here's what happens: What began as an *ideal* morphs into an *idol*. And we end up worshiping this ideal-turned-idol.

My ideal-turned-idol started innocently, as honest admiration and appreciation of Florence's ability to make her listeners double over with laughter. But then I wasted decades trying to strengthen a weakness and become someone I'm not.

I was so hyperfocused on trying to strengthen my weakness that when others expressed admiration and appreciation for how I'd shared my God-given strengths with them, I dismissed their genuine gratitude with a slew of *Yeah, buts*.

"You explained things so clearly, I feel like I finally understand!"
Yeah, but I wasn't funny.

"You challenged me to make a real change!"
Yeah, but I didn't make you laugh.

"You gave me new tools so I know what to do on Monday morning!"
Yeah, but I'm boring.

I used to call this humility. Now I recognize it as idolatry. Hyperfocusing on our weaknesses so we can be *just like her* is misplaced worship.

Now, I'm not suggesting we ignore our weaknesses; we need to take responsibility for them. But we can get so fixated on being *just like her* that we become oblivious to our God-given strengths.

Ask a group of Christian women to make a list of their weaknesses, and you'll hear a frenzy of pen scratching. Many will ask for more paper. But ask these same daughters of the King to brainstorm their strengths, and you'll be deafened by the silence.

Which must break our Creator's heart.

When Jesus Gets His Hands on Human Weakness

God doesn't ask us to overcome our weaknesses on our own. In fact, He does the exact opposite. Jesus demonstrates time and time again what happens when we give our weaknesses to Him.

Take the feeding of the five thousand, recorded in John 6:5–13, for example.

When Jesus looked up and saw a great crowd coming toward him, he said to Philip, "Where shall we buy bread for these people to eat?" He asked this only to test him, for he already had in mind what he was going to do.

Doesn't this sound like a trick question? As if Jesus is asking the impossible?

Philip answered him, "It would take more than half a year's wages to buy enough bread for each one to have a bite!"

Philip sounds a tad sarcastic . . . and totally overwhelmed.
He's saying, "Even if I worked for 180 days straight, I'd only earn enough money to feed all five thousand men ONE LITTLE BITE. Which is basically NOTHING. Because they'd want ANOTHER bite. And ANOTHER. And ANOTHER."
Feel at all familiar?
The feeling of *No matter how hard I work, no matter how much I do, I can't even make a dent!*

Another of his disciples, Andrew, Simon Peter's brother, spoke up, "Here is a boy with five small barley loaves and two small fish, but how far will they go among so many?"

Oh, how I identify with Andrew! And how I recognize the question that echoes in the heart of every woman awake at 2:37 a.m.: *How far will so little go among so many?*
How far will the few hours in my day go among so many tasks I need to do? How far will my feeble gifts go among all the people I care about? How far will my tiny attempts go among the endless needs I perceive?

Jesus said, "Have the people sit down." There was plenty of grass in that place, and they sat down (about five thousand men were there).

113

Jesus does nothing by accident. And John is a detail-conscious writer who records the scene with intentionality. So why does Jesus ask everyone to sit down? And why does John tell us "there was plenty of grass in that place"? This moment evokes Psalm 23:

> The Lord is my shepherd; I shall not want.
> He maketh me to lie down in green pastures. . . .
> He restoreth my soul. . . .
>
> vv. 1–3 KJV

And it sets the stage for John 10:14, when Jesus will tell them, "I am the good shepherd."

> Jesus then took the loaves, gave thanks, and distributed to those who were seated as much as they wanted. He did the same with the fish.

Philip gives up. Andrew gives up. All they can see is how little they have. Jesus gives thanks. God takes the little He has and multiplies it from scarcity into abundance. Notice how Jesus gives thanks for what others have ridiculed, mocked, disdained, and dismissed?

> When they had all had enough to eat, he said to his disciples, "Gather the pieces that are left over. Let nothing be wasted." So they gathered them and filled twelve baskets with the pieces of the five barley loaves left over by those who had eaten.

Notice, too, that John does not report that everyone gets "just barely enough to keep from fainting."

Nope.

He records that they all have "enough to eat." ENOUGH. More than enough, in fact. Abundance. Bounty. Excess!

And notice how many baskets were left over?

Twelve.

One per disciple. Imagine Philip and Andrew, each carrying his own basket of leftovers, finally realizing, *God multiplies my meager into His much.*

And now imagine yourself, after all these years of trying to become *just like her,* finally realizing, *I don't have to fix my own weaknesses. I can hand them over to Jesus to handle. He will multiply my meager into His much.*

Exhale an extra long sigh of relief.

You can stop trying to change who you are and start being more of who you are.

Discovering Your God-Given Strengths

Now take a deep breath in—'cause we're going to take a journey of discovery together.

Maybe you've already taken All. The. Quizzes. (Amy and I have, too. We may even know which Disney Princesses we are. . . . Just sayin.')

But this one is different. You'll see why in just a bit.

Your first step is to take the Love Who You ARE Personality Quiz in the back of this book (page 215). Or go online to take it at Exhale-Book.com/Personality-Quiz.

Celebrating Your God-Given Strengths

Have the results for your primary personality type and your secondary personality type? Great! We're about to dive into what they mean in terms of losing who you're NOT and loving who you ARE.

I'm going to walk through all four personality types, listing their key strengths as well as their key weaknesses. But before you read any further, grab a pad of Post-it Notes. Use them to

1. cover up the two personalities that are not your primary or secondary
2. cover up the weaknesses sections for your primary and secondary personality type

Why?

Step 1 is an intentional way to lose who you're NOT. Step 2 is a conscious way to learn to love who you ARE.

And if you're ready to ask, "Cheri, are you suggesting that we should completely ignore our weaknesses?" the answer is no, of course not. It's neither practical nor responsible to pretend that your weaknesses don't exist. That's why you used Post-it Notes rather than a fat black Sharpie: You can always lift up the Post-it Notes as needed.

But here's the thing: Research shows that when learning a new skill, beginners need loads of encouragement; it's intermediate and advanced learners who benefit most from critique (and even then, only when they've asked for it). Most of us have black belts in knowing our weaknesses, but we're total newbies when it comes to understanding and appreciating our God-given strengths. That's why I'm urging you to stop obsessing over your weaknesses and start embracing your God-given strengths.

As you do, pray-cess these questions:

1. What's my earliest memory of using this strength?
2. When have others affirmed this strength in me?
3. In what ways have I dismissed this strength as less valuable than the one(s) I wished for?
4. How has God worked through this strength to bless others?
5. What is stopping me from fully embracing and enjoying this strength?

The 4 Basic Personality Types

The Connector

When you are living fully from your Connector strengths, you . . .

- make everyone feel welcome, wanted, included
- get other people excited and on board with a new project

- tell stories that make others double over laughing one minute and reach for Kleenex the next
- exude an upbeat, optimistic mood that's contagious
- turn any occasion into a party and keep any conversation going
- enjoy taking center stage and basking in the spotlight

When you are stuck in Connector weaknesses, you . . .

- don't notice that you're monopolizing the conversation
- overwhelm others with your larger-than-life personality
- may be judged as surface, trite, immature
- forget details: names, important dates, commitments, etc.
- may fudge the facts in order to concoct excuses
- can come across as attention-seeking

If you're the **Connector**, here's what you need to know:

You *are God's masterpiece.*
He has created **you** *anew in Christ Jesus,*
so **you** *can do the good things he planned for* **you** *long ago.*
Ephesians 2:10 NLT (paraphrased)

The Inspector

When you are living fully from your Inspector strengths, you . . .

- say things that make others think, *Wow. That was profound!*
- create works of exceptional beauty: an exquisite floral arrangement, a detailed painting, a flawless musical performance, a perfect soufflé
- make co-workers want to up their game when they see how you raise the bar
- cause others to ponder what matters most in life

117

- transform chaos into order via smart systems and careful checklists
- notice details: names, dates, favorite colors, pizza toppings, etc.

When you are stuck in Inspector weaknesses, you . . .

- can make others feel inferior, even stupid
- tend toward pessimism and faultfinding
- believe you're only hard on yourself (when in reality you're hard on everyone)
- are so wedded to your systems and checklists that you can't flex with changing circumstances
- research to the point of paralysis, becoming overinformed and unable to make a choice that leads to action
- resent others for failing to notice important details in your life the way you do for them

If you're the **Inspector**, here's what you need to know:

You *are God's masterpiece.*
He has created you *anew in Christ Jesus,*
so you *can do the good things he planned for* you *long ago.*
Ephesians 2:10 NLT (paraphrased)

The Director

When you are living fully from your Director strengths, you . . .

- are the person others turn to when they need someone to take charge
- motivate people to take action RIGHT NOW
- just keep going and going and going . . . like the Energizer Bunny
- accomplish more than most people; your superpower is Getting Things Done

- crusade for justice; you are adamant about making change
- see the "big picture" and set your sights on a glorious, better future; you're a visionary

When you are stuck in Director weaknesses, you . . .

- take over, even when you haven't been invited to lead
- leave a trail of dead bodies in your wake as you forget people in your laser-focused pursuit of progress
- become a workaholic because you just keep going and going and going without stopping for restoration
- tend toward "Ready! Fire! Aim!"—no patience for long, drawn-out processes
- may be completely blindsided by surprises or sudden changes; you're used to being the one to cause change, not experience it
- can come across as arrogant because you tend to act independently rather than collaboratively

If you're the *Director*, here's what you need to know:

> **You** *are God's masterpiece.*
> *He has created* **you** *anew in Christ Jesus,*
> *so* **you** *can do the good things he planned for* **you** *long ago.*
> Ephesians 2:10 NLT (paraphrased)

The Reflector

When you are living fully from your Reflector strengths, you . . .

- take time to listen to others, making them feel seen and heard
- arbitrate during disagreements to help the differing factions recognize what they have in common and find a third alternative
- drop what you're doing to help someone in need
- exude a sense of calm confidence that helps others relax when they're around you

- try to understand others' perspectives even if they are different from your own
- value a life rhythm that prioritizes enough rest and simple routines

When you are stuck in Reflector weaknesses, you . . .

- switch from being fairly flexible to super stubborn when pushed too hard
- become passive; you'd rather do nothing than do the wrong thing
- abandon others, physically or emotionally, during major conflicts and crises
- procrastinate small annoying tasks, allowing them to grow into huge problems with major consequences
- avoid taking initiative or asking for help for so long that you end up needing to be rescued from a crisis
- may compromise your own needs, wants, and values for the sake of keeping the peace

If you're the *Reflector*, here's what you need to know:

You *are God's masterpiece.*
He has created **you** *anew in Christ Jesus,*
so **you** *can do the good things he planned for* **you** *long ago.*
Ephesians 2:10 NLT (paraphrased)

Receive Your Strengths

Learning to love who you ARE means . . .

- tearing down your secret idols
- refusing to *Yeah, but* your strengths while obsessing over your weaknesses

- celebrating your strengths as God's intentional expression of His character in and through you
- worshiping God—and only God—by fully living out the strengths He's given you

Scripture makes it clear: "Every good and perfect gift is from above" (James 1:17).

Your strengths are God's gifts to you. He doesn't force you to accept them. You must choose to receive them. Everything changes when you do.

When you receive what is yours, you won't "need" what is *not*.

You won't fall for the lie that it's selfish to embrace and enjoy who God created you to be. You'll stop trying to change who you are and— taking a big, brave breath—start being more of who you are.

You'll remember that you're the beloved daughter of our creator King. And you'll realize that loving who you ARE isn't a luxury that only other women get to enjoy.

It's your birthright, too.

now breathe

Write key words about your personality strengths on Post-it Notes and stick them where you'll see them often. When you do, pray-cess how you can use that strength to honor God, serve people, and enjoy being you today.

LOVE WHO YOU ARE:

You ARE gifted with God-given strengths.

eleven

Love Your Quirks: Because What Makes You Weird Is Wonderful

Amy

As I looked around me, I could scarcely take in a home so different from my own. I was at the house of Raju, a diminutive man, wrinkled as an apple doll, who has spent his whole life impoverished in India. Along with the rest of the community that he leads, he spends his days sifting through a local dump, looking for materials to retrieve and recycle.

Riding down the crowded roads of the Indian countryside on the way to Raju's community, the Mission India staff shared his story with us. Orphaned as a child, Raju had bounced from place to place enduring every abuse that we can imagine and many we don't want to. He was wired with a deep sense of justice, so these wrongs incensed him, fueling an anger he didn't know how to manage. Protesting turned into violence, which led to jail. Raju lived one grim reality after another until a pastor visiting the jail led him to Jesus.

Following Jesus changed his heart's trajectory, even though it didn't change his financial situation much. When I visited him, Raju's house was made of a hodgepodge of things he had salvaged from the dump where he scavenges. The walls were draped plastic, old blankets, and sheets. Metal bicycle rims, tires, and rusty car parts secured the tarp roof of his large tent home. Thin blankets on the floor were the seats for the families who came to meet with our team, but we were given plastic chairs of hospitality and honor.

Raju circulated in the midst of the crowd that gathered, smiling and greeting both his guests and the members of his tiny community— the families that he not only loves but also pastors and teaches in the church and the Mission India literacy class that meet in his home.

When everyone had gathered, Raju stood in the front and greeted us through an interpreter before he began to pray. Bowing his head, he started a stream of words that I couldn't understand, but later we were told that he was praying a blessing over us. All I knew was that I was suddenly overcome.

Unbidden, tears streamed down my face, and I had to steel myself against the sobs that threatened to rack my body. Through the sweep of emotion, I asked myself, *What's going on here? I can't even understand what he's saying. Why do I feel such awe and brokenheartedness?*

As I questioned, I began to feel the weight of God's Spirit that filled the room. I can't explain it. It just *was.* In the midst of the deepest poverty I've ever seen, I also experienced the most powerful, tangible presence of God that I've ever encountered. As Raju prayed, it was truly as if God sat in the room with us.

Suddenly, a tent made of trash became a tabernacle for the very presence of God.

What to Do with a Quirk

Raju has quite a list of characteristics that set the world against him. Like the Canaanite woman's circumstances, many of them are outside of his control. He's small-statured in a world that values height. In the Indian caste system, Raju is classified as a Dalit, or "untouchable," the class of people his culture considers subhuman. He's poor, and he doesn't hold a degree, both intrinsic traits of the community into which he was born.

But it's his passion for justice, part of his inner wiring, that earned him a police record. God created Raju to love justice even though it was something that got him into trouble at the beginning of his life.

Seeing how God works through Raju challenged me to look again at how God works through me. Many traits that I want to eliminate are the ones that God has redeemed and is using. He's refining my quirks—the traits He wove into me that sometimes make me feel weird or unwelcome—for His purposes. God has used both Raju's external circumstances and his internal wiring for His glory, a lesson not lost on this college-educated, middle-class, American woman.

In me, I see a chatterbox who needs to tame her tongue, but God sees a speaker. I see a woman who has a hard time keeping up with church-lady talk, but God sees authenticity that His girls need. I see a passion for justice that runs wild and gets me in trouble. God sees a strong voice for the weak. When we look through our Redeemer's lens, our quirks become our strengths.

Jesus never lets a past or an outcast status deter Him. After saying, "Follow me," He employs the gifts we'd rather hide. If that weren't true, Matthew, one of Jesus's twelve chosen disciples, never would have made the cut.

As I've studied, I've fallen for Matthew hard, and I hope you will, too. Here's the only little slice we see of his life with Jesus:

> As Jesus went on from there, he saw a man named Matthew sitting at the tax collector's booth. "Follow me," he told him, and Matthew got up and followed him.
>
> While Jesus was having dinner at Matthew's house, many tax collectors and sinners came and ate with him and his disciples. When the Pharisees saw this, they asked his disciples, "Why does your teacher eat with tax collectors and sinners?"

On hearing this, Jesus said, "It is not the healthy who need a doctor, but the sick."

Matthew 9:9–12

Besides this same story told by Luke, the only other time we see Matthew's name is in the other gospels when he's listed among the disciples and once in Acts. That's all. It's just one little story, but we can glean big truths.

Matthew the Quirky

None of the other disciples were leaders or influential people, but Matthew was a *tax collector*, a profession that made him an actual outcast. In contrast with the Canaanite woman who had "disqualifiers" beyond her control, tax collecting was Matthew's chosen profession, and it was a doozy. If you want to see the comic relief in the New Testament, just take a look at how many times "tax collectors and sinners" is repeated. Those guys were in a sin category all their own!

Can you imagine how the other disciples responded when Jesus added Matthew to their lot? My friend Suzie Eller made me snort-laugh when I read her imagined account of a conversation between God and Jesus in her book *Come with Me* that goes like this:

God: What about Simon Peter?

Jesus: He's one of the older guys, but he's a little impetuous.

God: Have you considered the brothers, James and John?

Jesus: Sometimes the brothers have their own best interests at heart.

God: What about Matthew?

Jesus: Wow, Matthew . . . I'm not sure anyone will understand that choice.[1]

1. Suzanne Eller, *Come with Me: Discovering the Beauty of Following Where He Leads* (Minneapolis: Bethany House, 2016), 40.

It's safe to say that Matthew wasn't the obvious choice. But let's take a look at a list of how Jesus actually used Matthew's quirks to qualify him.

Matthew's Meticulous Nature

Matt's tax-collector status may have had drawbacks, but the guy was evidently great at numbers and spreadsheets. Surprisingly, God uses these traits He created in Matthew for a new, redeemed purpose. Several commentators explain that Matthew's organizational and meticulous record-keeping talents honed in the tax-collecting business prepared him for writing a gospel.

Because he spent time with Jesus, taking note of every interaction, Matthew is the author of a book in the Bible. As J. C. Ryle says, "He wrote a book, which is known all over the earth. He became a blessing to others, as well as blessed in his own soul. . . . As long as the world stands, millions will know the name of Matthew, the publican."[2] The very gift Matthew had previously used for evil was ultimately used in a way that benefited both himself and the world.

If it weren't for Matthew's administrative skills, we'd have a weaker account of Jesus. His gospel declares Jesus as the long-awaited Messiah, the One who fulfills the prophecies. His gospel has the most ties to the Old Testament to help us see how God never changes and how He always keeps His promises.

Matthew's Ill-Gotten Gains

One of the reasons tax collectors were so hated among their people is that they almost always stole extra money to enrich themselves. Matthew's wealth might have been built on the backs of his Jewish community, but once he followed Jesus, all became His. Jesus turns Matthew's love of money from greed to generosity.

2. J. C. Ryle, *Expository Thoughts on the Gospels*, vol. 1 (Grand Rapids, MI: Baker Book House, 2007), 85.

Although Matthew modestly leaves out this detail in his own account, Luke shares that Matthew "held a great banquet for Jesus at his house" (Luke 5:29). The original word for *banquet*, or *feast* as used in other translations, describes a large reception with many guests. It's the kind of party that only a rich person could throw, a party with swag. Once he followed Jesus, Matthew lavished all his resources on Him. Not only that, but Matthew used his gift of financial resources to bring others to meet Jesus.

Matthew's Sketchy Friends

There's something that delights me about the way Matthew, a new follower who didn't know the churchy way to do things, invites all his outcast friends to meet Jesus. The funny thing is that Jesus seems delighted, too! In order to jolt my brain awake, I love to lay *The Message* side-by-side with my usual NIV translation. At the end of the story in this modern-language version, Jesus rebukes the Pharisees by saying, "I'm here to invite outsiders, not coddle insiders" (Matthew 9:13). Matthew used his sketchy connections to draw more needy people to Jesus. I'd say that's redemption right there.

Not one word that Matthew spoke was recorded, only his actions. He jumped to leave his old life, invited friends into his new one, and contributed to a book that I hold in my hands almost every morning. Matthew led a missional life, and that's why I've come to love him so. He isn't one of the flashy disciples. Matthew's story is small, but his eternal impact was big.

Following Matthew's Lead

Women often bury their most unique personality traits because they're "weird" or unpopular. These can actually be the winsome gifts the world needs. When the world sees you in all your God-created glory with every gift employed, they have a better understanding of the glory of God himself.

Matthew gives us a pattern that we can use to carefully unwrap the gifts God gave us . . . but which we don't necessarily value. The ones that make us different. The ones that can make us feel like an outsider. These are the very gifts that God wants redeemed and put on display for His glory. Let's follow Matthew through these steps, letting God show us our quirks in a whole new light.

Abandon the Norm to Follow Jesus

Without hesitation, Matthew left everything sure—everything familiar and safe—to follow Jesus. If we pause to think about Matthew's life, he surely had settled for "the devil he knew." It couldn't have been pleasant to be known as a bad-guy tax collector in his community. Yet there he sat in the booth, possibly enduring the glares and jeers of his people. He had to employ a God-given gift of faith to leave behind what he knew.

My hero from the beginning of the chapter, Raju, models Matthew's path for me. He definitely left the norm in India, where only 2.3 percent of the population is Christian and where choosing Jesus opens you up to hostility and persecution. He didn't choose the easy way, but he definitely chose the better way. Raju's been drawn close to God like all of us who follow Jesus—like Matthew, like you, like me.

Inertia can get the best of us, can't it? Even if life doesn't feel so great right now, moving forward can seem too hard. The difficulty of hiding your gifts behind a facade to fit in feels less scary than authenticity. Even if it's painful to shelve your gifts, it's less excruciating than being shamed for your superpower.

Without fail, Jesus calls us away from something when He calls us to himself. The blessings that follow when we leave our pursuit of "normal," however, are beyond compare, so we put to use the gift of whatever tiny grain of faith we have. We follow Him, which means offering up our gifts.

Make a Ruckus to Make a Difference

While it's true that Matthew threw a party like none other to honor Jesus, others thought his guest list should have been more carefully vetted. Those ever-critical Pharisees couldn't help themselves, saying, "What kind of example is this from your Teacher, acting cozy with crooks and riffraff?" (Matthew 9:11 MESSAGE).

Tapping into his gift of messy connections, Matthew violated social norms to invite his lost friends to meet Jesus. He makes quite a ruckus in the process.

Raju did the same. When the water truck, the only source of hydration for his village, skipped delivery for days on end, Raju made a bold move to win a basic right for his people. The truck finally showed up just as the people were thirsting to the brink of death. Raju pulled the driver out of the front seat, sending him back to town on foot. The driver was told that he would get his truck back after the village got a well, and *a well was installed.* Raju put his passionate gift for social change to work. With the help of Living Water, he got lifesaving water for his people.

A saying on a T-shirt I saw has become a favorite of mine. The shirt reads, "Women who behave rarely make history." As a southern girl, I can tell you that for far too long I put a premium on nice and normal.

One of my quirks that God is shaping to use is my longing for justice. It probably won't land me in a history book (and hopefully won't land me in the clinker), but maybe that's why my heart connected with Raju so strongly. We're twinning!

For decades I've been silent about issues I care about to keep the peace with others around me, but God is awakening a latent passion. I'm using my writing gifts to write blog posts about issues that deserve a new look through a biblical lens. I'm using my speaking gifts to leverage my voice for change. I'm using my teaching gifts to weave in scriptural mini-lessons on social justice in my women's class at church.

In this new stage, I feel stretched and uncomfortable because my strengthened voice is pushing me out of an acceptance zone into a place where some won't understand me. But I also feel energized and alive. God is giving an old foible new life in me; He's made my quirk a perk.

Don't get me wrong. I'm not talking about glorifying sin or being obnoxious. But I'm urging myself and others to fearlessly follow Jesus, dusting off our unused gifts, speaking up for what's right, and investing our lives instead of just spending them. That kind of life lives a little on the edge—not for the sake of edginess, but all for the love of Jesus.

Let Jesus Join His Name with Yours

Matthew's name will be forever joined with Jesus's, because he used his gift of record keeping to write a book proclaiming Him as Messiah. Truly amazing.

I'm learning to bend my passionate words to Jesus's will to make a difference.

How will you embrace your quirks to follow Jesus? Will you bring the gifts He's woven through you into the light to be redeemed and used by Him?

It's been years since I sat in Raju's house in the cloud of God's power, but I've been reflecting on it ever since. Raju isn't a man our world would consider wise. He barely has a fifth-grade education from one year in a literacy class, yet he has partnered with Mission India to teach others to read.

He isn't physically strong, yet this wizened, tiny man leads his community with a fierceness and joy that none denies.

He doesn't have material wealth, but as a pastor, he daily leads his congregation to the riches of the King of Kings.

Seeing how God's Spirit is alive and active in Raju's life, activating his redeemed gifts for good, has taught me a critical lesson. God doesn't just tolerate the foolish, weak, and lowly. He *chooses* them.

❋ *now breathe*

Name a trait or two that once defined you that you've buried in order to fit in.

How might God want to use that gift for His glory today?

Call out a unique trait in a sister today. Be specific and complimentary.

LOVE WHO YOU ARE:

You ARE *beautifully quirky.*

Twelve

Love Your Gifts: Because You're Exactly What Your World Needs

Cheri

I don't belong here.

I pick up my notes from the podium to check the page numbers.

I still have nightmares of the time when the last page of my message went missing. But tonight, page 36 is right where it belongs.

A woman waltzes up the aisle to me, all smiles.

"You're Kathi Lipp's friend, aren't you!" she gushes. "She spoke here last year, and we all just loved her!"

I smile and open my mouth to respond, but she continues.

"She is so funny! She had us all rolling. Are you funny like Kathi?"

My face freezes for a long awkward moment. Finally, I muster up, "Well, you know, there's no one quite like Kathi!"

The woman's smile gives way to worry; she walks away.

I don't belong here.

I wipe my sweaty hands on my skirt.

God, you made a mistake in calling me here. They don't want me; they want someone funny, like Kathi. They don't want Nerdy Girl.

I resist the urge to run to the back table, scoop up my stacks of color-coded handouts, and dump them in the trash.

What was I thinking, bringing charts and diagrams?

My fingers feel the remote control in my pocket.

And dozens of PowerPoint slides? They don't want a lecture, they want entertainment!

With ten minutes on the clock until the Friday-night session begins, my mind races back in time to sixth grade. To the day when the two most popular girls in class passed notes that said "We don't like Cheri today" to all the other girls.

I look around the room at the women who have already claimed their seats and those who are streaming in.

What if they all decide they don't like me today? What if they all agree that I don't belong here?

When it's time for me to speak, I'm introduced as "coming highly recommended by Kathi."

I walk to the podium, straighten my notes, wipe my hands on my skirt, and ask, "How many of you have heard Kathi speak?"

The room erupts in applause and cheers.

"How many of you remember how funny she is?"

Again, the women clap with gusto.

"There's something you need to know, right up front," I begin, and then I wait for the uproar to die down before deadpanning, "I am nothing like Kathi."

The women start to laugh . . . until they realize that I'm serious. Then they don't know what to do.

Despite feeling *I don't belong here* more than ever, I do the only thing I can: I launch into the message God has given me to give to them.

Complete with handouts and PowerPoint slides.

After the session is over, women come to tell me:

"That was exactly what I needed to hear!"

"Your slides were so powerful! They really drove your point home."

"Can I take extra handouts home with me? I want to give them to some friends!"

Eventually, the room empties, except for one woman who has been waiting for me. She looks like the kind of grande dame I want to be when I grow up, eyes sparkling with mischief mingled with wisdom. She grabs me by one arm and pulls me close so she can dig me in the ribs with an elbow.

"You may not be as funny as Kathi," she declares, "but you're funny enough."

She winks and walks away.

And it hits me once again, as it has so many times: *I do belong here. God created me, and God called me; thus, I belong, despite the feelings that tempt me to believe otherwise.*

I walk back up to the podium to grab my notes and pause. *Before speaking, the "I don't belong here" feeling hit so hard, it felt like gospel truth.*

But now, I look out over the empty seats and remember the women taking notes, nodding, flipping through their Bibles, reaching for Kleenex, and even laughing.

I breathe out a deep sigh, not of relief but of profound gratitude. *God did not make a mistake. He knew what He was doing when He called me here.*

I inhale slowly, reminding myself, *To love who I am, I must trust His call.*

"What Is God Calling Me to Do?"

Perhaps you've never stepped up to a podium (with or without a PowerPoint presentation!).

But you do know what *I don't belong here* feels like, and you've had experience questioning God's call.

Perhaps you've wondered, *Do I even have a call from God? If so, what is He calling me to do?*

Maybe you've taken a spiritual gifts assessment (or two) in hopes of gaining clarity.

(You probably have not taken the same spiritual gifts assessment over and over, changing your answers each time in hopes of finally getting the results you want. I mean, who would do something crazy like that?)

When you see a list of spiritual gifts like this . . .

prophecy	healing	pastor
service (ministry)	miracles	celibacy
teaching	discerning of spirits	voluntary poverty
exhortation	tongues	martyrdom
giving	interpretation of	missionary
leadership	tongues	hospitality
mercy	apostle	intercession
wisdom	helps	deliverance
knowledge	administration	leading worship
faith	evangelist	

. . . it's natural to scrutinize it, in hopes the answer to your question "What is God calling me to DO?" will jump out at you.

Or maybe you're brand-new to spiritual gifts and can't wait to take an assessment—you'll find links to several at ExhaleBook.com.

But before tackling the question, "What is God calling me to do?" I invite you to turn to Scripture and ask, "How do I learn to trust God's call?" After all, to love who you are, you must trust His call.

Trusting God's Call

During my most recent trip through the book of John, I almost skipped chapter 10. After all, I've heard or read the story of the Good Shepherd. So. Many. Times.

But I had a new journaling Bible, with lined margins for writing, and a brand-new set of Bible highlighters in four colors.

And I couldn't stand to leave two full pages unmarked. So I decided to give chapter 10 a quick read-through, jot down some notes, highlight a few key words, and quickly move on.

Within the first few verses, however, I found myself rapidly switching between highlighters. And by verse 16, I'd come to a complete halt, surprised to have discovered a list I'd never noticed before. (It was a total *Who re-wrote the book?* moment.)

1. Listen to His voice
2. Know His voice
3. Follow Him
4. Be saved
5. Come in
6. Go out
7. Find pasture
8. Have life
9. Have life to the full
10. There shall be one flock and one Shepherd

Now, I'm not a fan of Top 10 Tips–type articles. The order is usually arbitrary rather than logical, and this inquiring mind wants to know why #1 is #1 and why #10 is #10. But the list I jotted in the margin of John 10:3–16 feels like a logical progression.

> The gatekeeper opens the gate for [the shepherd], and the sheep **listen** to his voice. He calls his own sheep by name and leads them out.

The first thing we do is **listen**. Actively, not passively. We aren't lying around to see if our Shepherd is worth listening to today. The Shepherd and us, we have this routine down. He invites us, by name, and goes ahead to escort us out. For us, hearing means action.

> When he has brought out all his own, he goes on ahead of them, and his sheep **follow** him because they **know** his voice. But they

will never follow a stranger; in fact, they will run away from him because they do not recognize a stranger's voice.

Because of our daily interactions, we **know** our Shepherd's voice; we recognize Him even in the dark. When we hear His voice, we **follow** Him with absolute certainty, confident that He is our Leader.

If we hear anyone else's voice, we recognize danger and escape.

(Except, of course, when I listen to strangers when I should be scared of them, and follow them when I should be fleeing. Or when I listen to the voice of condemnation within—so familiar, so subtle, that it often goes unrecognized as a "stranger." All of which results in me needing rescue, which we'll discuss in chapter 14.)

I am the gate; whoever enters through me will **be saved.**

When faced with danger, we are saved by our Shepherd. He rescues us. What a brave Shepherd!

They will **come in** and **go out,** and find **pasture.**

We enjoy in-and-out privileges, and the pasture our Shepherd takes us to is lush and vast. We are surrounded with abundance!

The thief comes only to steal and kill and destroy; I have come that they may **have life,** and **have it to the full.** . . . I am the good shepherd; I know my sheep and my sheep know me—just as the Father knows me and I know the Father—and I lay down my life for the sheep.

There are villains in our lives whose goal is to sacrifice us to get what they want. In contrast, our Shepherd's goal is to sacrifice himself to give us life. And not an ordinary life, but life to the full—beyond anything we could expect!

I have other sheep that are not of this sheep pen. I must bring them also. They too will listen to my voice, and **there shall be one flock and one shepherd.**

Finally, when our Shepherd calls and we respond, we are one flock, and He is our one Shepherd.

We listen to Him; we belong together.

One Call Fits All

This is the bottom-line answer to "What is God calling you to do?": Be one flock with one Shepherd.

God has given you spiritual gifts to build up the body of Christ (1 Corinthians 12:27) and unify believers in "the bond of peace" (Ephesians 4:3). Exactly how we contribute to the one flock with one Shepherd will look different for each of us. Here are a few questions and examples to help you get started:

1. What clues does my childhood hold?
   When I look back at my childhood, I see:

   - As a toddler, I used to line up my stuffed toys in my crib and "read" aloud to them.
   - When I was five, I came home from my first piano lesson and promptly taught my friend from across the street everything I'd just learned and ordered her to go home and practice— which she did! (Yes, "Action Amy" and I are both Directors!)
   - During the summer after fourth grade, my mother told me I could do whatever I wanted with the spare bedroom in our house; naturally, I turned it into a classroom, complete with desks, bulletin boards, and textbooks.
   - When I was in junior high, I started teaching the weekly Bible lesson in the primary class. During summers, I taught at Vacation Bible School.

2. What errors can I simply not ignore?
   I constantly stifle the urge to correct grammar and punctuation. Everywhere. All the time. I do keep a red pen, a black

Sharpie, and Wite-Out in my purse, just in case people ask for my help . . . or I see a sign that needs to be corrected on the sly.

I also have to bite my tongue when someone mispronounces words during casual conversation. I consciously remind myself that as long as I understand what they mean, they're communicating, it's all good. But I still wince a little (hopefully just on the inside!).

And when people don't know what I know, I just have to share it with them, whether it's by forwarding a fascinating article or talking their ear off about the book I'm currently reading. I'm driven to correct ignorance, not out of condescension but because knowledge brings me joy that I want to share!

3. What expertise have people come to expect from me?
My friends have been coming to me with questions like, "What does this word mean?" and "What verb tense should I use here?" and "Do I need to use an apostrophe?" and "How can I change this sentence so it says what I mean?" as far back as junior high.

I've spent a quarter of a century in classrooms ranging from sixth grade to college, teaching English, reading, composition, and speech.

Nowadays, coaching clients come to me lamenting, "I'm a speaker, not a writer!" and "I flunked English class!" and "I'm no good at grammar/spelling/punctuation/etc." When I'm asked to give an article or book chapter "The Full Cheri Gregory" treatment, I'm delighted to collaborate with the author. They expect me to draw from all my expertise and experience to make sure their unique voice comes through clearly in their written message.

Yes, teaching is one of my primary spiritual gifts. Just try to make small talk with me over hors d'oeuvres at a dinner party, and you'll get a full-blown lecture—complete with PowerPoint if my cell phone has good Wi-Fi access.

One Goal, Different Roles

Here's where things get really interesting.

Amy has the spiritual gift of teaching, too. I know firsthand what a superb teacher she is, because she was my speaking coach for several years. But because the distribution of her other spiritual gifts differs from mine, we have vastly different teaching styles. We can work together without worrying about duplication, knowing that even in our area of overlap, we still complement each other rather than compete with each other.

We saw this so clearly when we started the *Grit 'n' Grace* podcast. Separately, we each went through a list of necessary podcasting tasks, rating each one on a scale of "I'd rather die than do this" to "This sounds like so much fun!" Anticipating the temptation to give accommodating, middle-of-the-road scores, we promised to be completely candid.

Before comparing our ratings, Amy confessed, "I feel so guilty because I cherry-picked all the good stuff for me to do." I assured her that I felt the same way. When we revealed our scores, we discovered that every single task she'd ranked low, I'd ranked high, and vice versa. We laughed with relief, grateful for God's masterful planning and clear confirmation of our collaboration.

When *You* Show Up

Even though I almost let my insecurities about my gifts derail me, the retreat at which I'm dubbed "funny enough" goes well. After the final session, when almost everyone has headed to the cafeteria for brunch, one woman approaches me.

"Do you have a second?" she asks.

"Sure!" I reply, expecting a question.

But her next words are as unexpected as they are unforgettable.

"You looked like you were thoroughly enjoying being yourself this weekend. I just wanted to tell you that watching you be yourself gave me permission to be myself, too."

She hugs me and leaves.

I stare after her, incredulous. Overwhelmed, I sit and inhale the unexpected truth of her words like oxygen.

When you love who you are, you give others permission to be who they are.

When you show up as yourself—created by God and called by God—you help others see what it means to belong to the body of Christ.

We belong to Him. We belong together.

And we need you to show up as you.

now breathe

Journal your answers to these questions as you pray-cess what God has called you to do and the spiritual gifts He's given you:

1. What clues does my childhood hold?
2. What errors can I simply *not* ignore?
3. What expertise have people come to expect from me?

LOVE WHO YOU ARE:

You ARE essential to the body of Christ.

Thirteen

Love Your Unique Calling: Because the World Is Waiting for You

Amy

"What do you want me to do for you?"

Close your eyes for a minute and picture it. Jesus is standing right in front of you, asking that question.

"What do you want me to do for you?"

How would you answer? The possibilities are limitless because He's limitless.

If I'm honest, some really shallow answers pop to mind first. I've always wanted a convertible. It would be nice to have the mortgage paid off. Wait . . . maybe I'll ask Jesus for the ability to never say the wrong thing again. That would be an awesome gift!

But then the deeper, nobler part of me takes over, and I start thinking about God's will and the indescribable pleasure of walking in step with Him. Ultimately, because I'm a woman who has come to know that His glory is for my highest good, my answer would be, "Tell me what to *do* to please you."

"Action Amy," a nickname I earned on a mission trip for my constant drive for activity, didn't begin as a compliment, but I've certainly lived up to it. It describes me exactly. I always want to know what to *do*!

I read Cheri's last chapter with tears. Yes! Our highest calling is to "be one flock with one Shepherd." Beautiful and true.

But what does that look like? How do we walk it out in our everyday lives? Once we lose who we're not, creating margin by saying no to all the things that have kept us tied up in knots . . . and once we love who we are, identifying the gifts we've been given as God's unique daughters . . . now that we understand the higher calling to walk in unity with our Leader, what do we *do* with all that?

What Do You Want Me to Do for You?

Jesus only asked this extraordinary question twice, and we find accounts of both instances back-to-back in Mark 10. The first time, He asks James and John, otherwise known as the Sons of Thunder (that nickname sounds a little like the backhanded compliment of Action Amy, doesn't it?):

> Then James and John, the sons of Zebedee, came to him [Jesus]. "Teacher," they said, "we want you to do for us whatever we ask."
> "What do you want me to do for you?" he asked.
>
> Mark 10:35–36

Amazing, right? Can you imagine how excited the brothers were? Jesus encouraged them to ask for whatever they wanted, and now they come back with this stunning request: "Let one of us sit at your right and the other at your left in your glory" (v. 37).

Epic. Fail. In His grace, Jesus tells them that they have no idea what they're asking for and that the Father is the decision-maker on that one. Disappointment is the inevitable result when we ask Jesus for the wrong thing.

Just verses later, we see Jesus ask the same question again with a very different outcome.

> Then they came to Jericho. As Jesus and his disciples, together with a large crowd, were leaving the city, a blind man, Bartimaeus (which means "son of Timaeus"), was sitting by the roadside begging. When he heard that it was Jesus of Nazareth, he began to shout, "Jesus, Son of David, have mercy on me!"
> Many rebuked him and told him to be quiet, but he shouted all the more, "Son of David, have mercy on me!"
> Jesus stopped and said, "Call him."
> So they called to the blind man, "Cheer up! On your feet! He's calling you." Throwing his cloak aside, he jumped to his feet and came to Jesus.
> "What do you want me to do for you?" Jesus asked him.
>
> vv. 46–51

So much is happening in this tiny passage, but two facts that I uncovered rocked me as I studied. First, Bartimaeus calls Jesus "Son of David" even though the passage tells us that the crowd introduced Him as "Jesus of Nazareth." Although Bartimaeus is physically blind, he already has spiritual sight. He knows that Jesus is the Messiah, not just a man.

Second, the word for "mercy" is *eleos* in the original language. *Eleos* can also be translated as "alms." Bartimaeus's cry is the plea for pocket change heard from all beggars of the day, so Jesus's question is a clarifying question. In essence, Jesus is asking, "What do you want from me? Do you just want money, or are you seeking something more?"

Clarifying Calling

Finally, the repetition of the words *call* and *calling* stopped me in my tracks. At the sound of Bartimaeus's cries, Jesus halts and responds, "Call him," and the crowd that had moments before been shushing Bartimaeus now joyfully says, "He's calling you!"

144

The very word *calling* is fraught, isn't it? It feels like a word saved for special people and for people paid to do ministry. One dictionary definition of *calling* is "a profession or occupation," but the one we most commonly think of is "a strong urge toward a particular way of life or career." Christians identify God as the source of that strong urge, so *calling* sometimes takes on a mystical aura that seems too big for us.

But here Jesus calls a very ordinary man. In fact, Bartimaeus would have been considered subordinate by a culture that prejudged the infirm as sinful. His blindness could have been a barrier, yet when Jesus calls, Bartimaeus comes.

Even beyond the thought that calling is too mysterious, we have additional obstacles between us and God's call. Sometimes doubt keeps us stuck, wondering if we really heard God or dreamed up our newest harebrained scheme on our own. We can even doubt that God would want to use us.

Sometimes we can be tripped up in the church world when calling is used as a subtle manipulation toward human expectation. Calling becomes based on a skewed ideology instead of sound theology—for example, saying that all women are called to be wives.

Another stumbling block to calling is self-doubt, feeling certain that *she's* better or more equipped. Comparison kills calling.

Some of us have let our callings die on the vine because of hard circumstances or the voices of naysayers or the diversion of busyness in our day-to-day lives. The dreams we once held dear have faded away until they're fuzzy and distant. Doubt, false ideals, comparison, and dying dreams are obstacles to calling that we've probably all faced at different stages of life.

The truth is, however, that Jesus calls each one of us. He draws us close and calls us His brothers and sisters (Matthew 12:50). He erases the divide of His divinity and calls us friends (John 15:15). Just the way Jesus called Bartimaeus to come to Him, He calls us. Our first calling is simply to be near Him.

Once Bartimaeus comes close, Jesus asks the big question, "What do you want me to do for you?"

> The blind man said, "Rabbi, I want to see."
> "Go," said Jesus, "your faith has healed you."

Mark 10:51–52

Bartimaeus didn't take a play from the Sons of Thunder's book. He didn't ask for position. Instead, Bartimaeus asked for wholeness, and because of his faith, Jesus granted it. When we have spiritual sight, we ask for the right things. Only when we've grasped the spiritual gift are we ready for the physical gift.

Bartimaeus asked for the right thing, a gift richer than money, and Jesus granted his request, not only with healing but by giving him something to do. "Go!" Jesus said, and Bartimaeus did. "Immediately he received his sight and followed Jesus along the road" (v. 52).

Where exactly did Bartimaeus go? We don't know for sure, but there's a tiny hint embedded in this passage. Matthew 20 records this same healing account, but Matthew reports two blind men receiving their sight. Mark only focuses on one, and he gives us his name, Bartimaeus. Scholars suggest that Mark may have focused exclusively on Bartimaeus and named him because he was still part of the early church when Mark wrote his account of his days with Jesus. If that's true, then Bartimaeus went with the crowd, followed Jesus to the cross, and became part of the body of Christ after Jesus's resurrection. "Go!" was Jesus's calling, and Bartimaeus embraced it. He became part of one flock following one Shepherd.

What's Your "Go"?

Bartimaeus was called. I'm called. You're called. We're all called, not because we're outstanding but because we belong to Jesus. A big part

146

of His calling is *being*, learning to exhale and become our truest God-created self. As my niece Megan has said, "God's definition of calling is a gentle, steady, beautiful pull, not a threat."

The other part of that calling, however, is doing. Ephesians 2:10 tells us, "For we are God's handiwork, created in Christ Jesus to do good works, which God prepared in advance for us to do." In essence, calling is first drawing close to Jesus and then going, being sent out in His Spirit to do His work.

It's particularly difficult to know what we're called to do when our days, hours, and minutes were previously filled with what everybody else wanted us to do. Or what we *thought* they wanted us to do. Or what we thought they needed.

Also, there's no single calling for our life. There's a lifetime of callings, different ones for each season, but how do we find our "go" right now? When it's time to find our place in the one flock with one Shepherd, there's a process that leads us to the right spot.

Glance Back

If you're not sure of your current calling, you probably already have more informational indicators than you know.

God doesn't waste anything. Psalm 23:3 says, "He guides me along the right paths for his name's sake." We can let out a huge sigh of relief right here. We may think that we've strayed from the path, been pushed from the path, or taken a nose dive off the path, but all those paths are redeemed for His glory.

It's useful to create an inventory of what our past holds. I love the way Cheri got us started by thinking about clues from our childhood. A list of past jobs and roles, including volunteer positions or caretaker functions, can also shed light on patterns God has put in your life.

Also think about the skills you used in those jobs. Do you see repetition or overlap? As you glance at your past, ask God to show you

His hand in guiding you to the next thing. Our past can hold clues to our current calling.

Peer Forward

My little-girl heart held dreams of being on stage as I sang into the hairbrush held in my hand. Although nobody is going to hire me to sing (seriously, don't do it), I now get hired to stand on a stage to speak. Having a captive audience is the fulfillment of my dearest dreams. (Wink! Wink!)

What dreams for the future have you held in your heart? Like my dream to be a pop star, your dream might not come true in its original form, but I'm a huge believer that our dreams, the deepest desires of our hearts, give us an indication of God's calling. Psalm 37:4, "Take delight in the Lord, and he will give you the desires of your heart," holds delicious promise, but I don't believe that it means that we get anything that we want. It means that when we prioritize God, He plants His desires within us. Make a list of the dreams that you've had since childhood, including those you've put aside, and consider how those dreams might be pointing to your "go."

Look Around

After glancing at the past and peering into the future, let's ground ourselves firmly in today. Your path has prepared you for your present. All our past experiences fueled by our dreams help us to identify our calling and know what to do right now.

I was in a huge transition almost a decade ago, and I felt stuck. After leaving the classroom to care for our sons at home, I always contributed in some way to our family's finances through working part-time. I'd held a variety of jobs—keeping a child in our home, teaching adult education classes, writing for our tiny local newspaper, and even visiting new-comers to our community through a company like Welcome Wagon.

But since all of those jobs had come to a natural end, I went back to teaching for a year. One. Miserable. Year. Even though I had been zealous about teaching before my kids were born, the misery I felt going back to it made me realize that it was no longer my calling. What's a girl to do when what's she's doing isn't working? I pouted and prayed. I threw things, and I thought.

One weekend in the midst of wrestling with God, looking for what was next and feeling frustrated by no obvious endgame, my friend Holly traveled with me to a speaking event. We chatted as we road-tripped, and Holly started asking me about my experience with the speaker team on which I serve. One question was all it took to start me gushing about the love, support, and mentoring I was receiving.

"Most women in ministry aren't part of a team. I wonder what they do?" she asked after a small, quiet pause.

In that moment, in what I can only describe as a nearly audible click, the idea for Next Step Coaching Services was born. I could help those lonely women. I knew I could! Glancing back at my past, I had teaching experience in many kinds of classrooms, as well as business experience from my welcome-service job. Through that service as well as through my speaking for churches, I had been honing my skills for over six years. My biggest dream was to have a job where I could talk about Jesus every day and have greater impact for Him. Continuing to help provide for my family was the essential but yummy icing on the cake.

"Go!" Jesus breathed into that moment with my friend Holly, and I did. I'm still going, coaching other speakers, as I write this book.

My current calling isn't pie-in-the-sky or detached from my every-day life, and neither is yours. My family's financial needs are relevant, and yours are important, too. We've made this idea of calling over-complicated and ethereal, when God simply wants us to listen to His voice, look at the gifts He's given us, include the practical in His provision, and act. And the most beautiful part is that God also gives us something that we're created to love. Following God's calling is rarely easy, but it's often simpler than we've made it.

Jesus's Question and Our Calling

When Jesus asks us, "What do you want me to do for you?" we can look back at James, John, and Bartimaeus for insight and principles on what to *do* now.

- Do ask for perception, not position.
- Do "go," joining Jesus on the journey.
- Do stay and serve. (One flock. One Shepherd. See how this works? So exciting!)

Calling isn't just for "special people." It isn't separate from regular life and paying the bills. Rather, it's integrated into who we are at our core. Calling isn't mysterious, selfish, or unattainable.

Calling is for each one of us, and it starts with coming close to Jesus. He's calling us today to be His, to be part of His people, and to do His work. It's time, and there's no one else to fill your spot. Let's use all the progress we've made so far to run into our calling. The world is waiting.

now breathe

Do you know your current calling? If so, journal about how you were called and how you're "go"-ing.

If not, go to ExhaleBook.com, where you'll find a work sheet to help you glance at the past, peer into the future, and look around in order to seek God for your calling.

LOVE WHO YOU ARE:

You ARE *a woman with a current calling.*

fourteen

Love Your Humanity: Because It's Better to Be Lost and Found

Cheri

What went wrong?

It's Monday evening, and I'm driving back to my hotel after day one of a two-day workshop, trying to figure out why I'm in such a bad mood.

All morning I felt upbeat. The presentations were superb, in both content and style. But after lunch, my emotions took a downward plunge. And now I can't seem to turn them around.

Did I get a text message from home that's still bugging me? Was it something one of my peers said? Didn't say?

I open my heart in prayer. *What is this about, Lord? What am I not getting?*

The answer is immediate and startling.

"You didn't get his attention."

Ahhh, yes. The workshop instructor didn't really notice me.

"You didn't just want to be noticed. You wanted to impress him."

I frown. *I'm way too old to still be trying to impress my teachers.*

The next morning, my plans to arrive early are ruined by a GPS malfunction. Ten minutes late, I try to slip quietly into the front row of the workshop. But my purse strap hooks on a chair, yanking me off balance.

The instructor stops his presentation and stares straight at me. My cheeks burn. I stumble to my seat, pull out my computer, and start taking notes, hoping he'll ask a question so I can make up for my mistake.

Make up for my mistake? What, like extra credit?

Soon, he opens up a brainstorming session. Other attendees offer great answers. I evaluate mine against each of theirs and eventually put my hand halfway up.

"Ahhh, that's a powerful example!" he exclaims as he writes my suggestion on the whiteboard.

I flush again, this time with . . . pride? No, relief. *I've received what I need.*

As the warm glow fades, I look down and realize that I've not added my idea to my notes. And it dawns on me: *My idea wasn't for me. It was for him.*

I started trying to impress my teacher on the first day of kindergarten and never stopped. My school years felt like a series of auditions for the coveted lead role in every class: teacher's pet. I was a method actor, adjusting who I was based on what I knew would impress each teacher most. By high school, when I was taking seven different classes from seven different teachers, I was playing the parts of seven different students, switching personas in the hallway during the four-minute break between bells.

What matters most to me is impressing the teacher.

Not what I learn. Not who I become. I have a lifelong habit of trying to impress The Most Important Person in the Room. Because when it comes to dealing with people, years of experience have etched this cautionary mantra on my heart:

I can be myself, or I can be loved.

Impress or Acquiesce?

You've spent the last six chapters discovering that it's not just okay to be yourself: It's vital that you be yourself. God created you on purpose, for a purpose! You've committed to "Lose who you're NOT" and "Love who you ARE."

But it's one thing to decide, "Yes! I'm going to be exactly who God created me to be!" when you're reading a book all by yourself. And it's a very different thing to live out this decision when dealing with other people. Especially if you've been conditioned from an early age to identify The Most Important Person in the Room and to impress them . . . or acquiesce to them.

When you're a master at making a good impression, you can read the slight flicker in the eyes, the tilt of a head, the particular tone of voice. And you automatically respond by shapeshifting, becoming who "they" want and need you to be in any given moment.

Or maybe you acquiesce rather than impress. You figure out The Most Important Person in the Room and stay as far off their radar as possible. You hide in the back row. Aim to slip in and out unnoticed. Do everything you can to disappear into the woodwork.

Either way, dealing with people has proved what you've always suspected: You can be yourself, *or* you can be loved.

The Drawbacks of Impressing

If you've thrown yourself into earning love by impressing others, their approval may not be quite the same thing as love, but it can feel like a close second. Approval seems attainable, like something you can control with enough impression management.

Unfortunately, impressing comes with serious drawbacks.

1. Being impressive makes you dismissive

The first time I encountered a teacher I couldn't impress was the first day of my senior year of high school.

Mr. B was new to the school I'd attended since kindergarten. He had the audacity to introduce himself to the honors algebra class as someone who had "always been a C student."

I remember thinking, *This is not how to make a good first impression.* Glancing around to see if my classmates were similarly shocked, I wondered, *How come someone like him is teaching us? This is a class of students who earn As, not Cs.*

As an honor roll student, I was used to being among the best of the best. But try as I might, I couldn't get a read on Mr. B that day. It didn't sound like acing tests or earning extra credit was going to earn me his good graces. He kept saying strange stuff like, "Failure is a normal part of the learning process," "Your growth is more important than your grades," and other nonsense.

I was so unimpressed. I sat back in my seat, crossed my arms across my chest, and shook my head, thinking, *What can I possibly learn from him?*

You might be thinking, *Oh, that's so typical of an immature teenager.* But sadly, this judgmental attitude followed me into my adult years. Because the flip side of trying to earn love by being impressive is judging unimpressive people as unlovable.

So you write people off without recognizing what you're doing. Sometimes, you're so busy trying to impress The Most Important Person in the Room that you're not really aware of anyone else who is there.

2. Being impressive makes you invulnerable

When you're caught up in impression management, everyone sees you as the last woman on earth who might possibly need help. And you don't ask for help because you can't recognize (let alone admit) *neediness.*

Perish the thought.

You pride yourself on needing nothing: no handouts, no helping hands. You are the rescu*er,* not the rescu*ed,* thank you very much!

And you back all of this up with Scriptures in which Jesus himself said, "Impress people with all your heart and with all your soul and with all your strength and with all your mind" and "This is my command: that you impress one another."

Ahem.

Jesus's words are clear: "Love the Lord your God with all your heart and with all your soul and with all your strength and with all your mind" (Luke 10:27) and "Love one another" (John 13:34).

You know, in your head, that these words are true.

But you also know from years of experience how much easier it is to impress The Most Important Person in the Room than to love everyone in any room.

Love is great—in theory. But in action, love is messy. People are complicated and uncooperative. They don't come with instruction manuals, or even cheat sheets. So you never know if you're getting it right, even when you mean well and do your best.

What Love Looks Like

Fortunately, we have a guide. Jesus—the Most Important Person in any room—offers this vivid picture of what love looks like in action:

> Suppose one of you has a hundred sheep and loses one of them. Doesn't he leave the ninety-nine in the open country and go after the lost sheep until he finds it?
>
> And when he finds it, he joyfully puts it on his shoulders and goes home. Then he calls his friends and neighbors together and says, "Rejoice with me; I have found my lost sheep."
>
> I tell you that in the same way there will be more rejoicing in heaven over one sinner who repents than over ninety-nine righteous persons who do not need to repent.
>
> Luke 15:4–7

And here is where I have a confession to make: I've spent my life externally saying, "What a beautiful parable this is!" and "Yes, of course, the lost sheep represents me, a sinner."

But in my heart, I didn't mean it.

After all, I've spent my life doing what's supposed to be done. The way it should be done. And for heaven's sake, I've made sure that I am always where I'm supposed to be, when I'm supposed to be there.

The last thing I want is anyone having to come look for me!

Oh, I've paid lip service to being a lost sheep.

But my life has demonstrated that I like to consider myself part of the 99 who do not need to repent.

The 99 Club

What I *really* want is membership in The 99 Club. After all, the unwritten rules of The 99 Club are comfortingly familiar:

- Do it all.
- Hold everything together.
- Show no weakness.

And above all else?

- Impress The Most Important Person in the Room.

Being part of The 99 Club means that nobody has to look for me, nobody has to find me, nobody has to carry me, and I don't have to repent for anything.

Ever.

Which all sounds oh-so-impressive.

Of course, to be a member of The 99 Club, I'd have to avoid Jesus.

He seeks the lost. He welcomes sinners and eats with them. He reaches out to people I find easy to dismiss.

And I dislike the unimpressive names Jesus has for those who get really excited about membership in The 99 Club: "fools . . . hypocrites . . . blind guides . . . whitewashed tombs . . . snakes . . . brood of vipers" (Matthew 23:17–33).

156

But most of all, as a member of The 99 Club, I do not like how Jesus treats "the one."

No, I do not.

Neither do the rest of us in The 99 Club. We all agree that it's scandalous. It breaks all of our rules for Jesus to seek the one. So joyfully. To put the errant sheep on His shoulders. Take it home. Call up His friends and neighbors and invite them to rejoice.

And not just rejoice: To add insult to injury, there is more rejoicing over the one than over those of us who stay put in The 99 Club. If we're honest, we find ourselves thinking, *This is so unfair. It is not right to reward failure. What about me? What about all I've done for Him?!*

When we entertain such thoughts, we fail to see how far we have wandered from Jesus. Any time we are muttering bitterly in our hearts, "What about all I've done for Him?!" we are more lost than we can possibly imagine.

And we are in the midst of the worst kind of failure: heart failure.

The One Club

Of course, not a one of us has membership in The 99 Club. Not a one of us is beyond the need for repentance. Each one of us wanders. Each one of us becomes lost. Each one of us is "the one" Christ came to seek.

Each one of us belongs to The One Club. The One Club has vastly different rules from The 99 Club. In fact, it has only one rule: *Be yourself.*

Belonging to The One Club means that you can be yourself *and* be loved.

In fact, you can't really experience love unless you are yourself. Because you can only fully receive love that's meant for you. The real you. The messy you. The unimpressive you. The you that wanders off and gets lost. The you in constant need of rescue.

When you recognize how lost you've been, you feel such relief at being found.

Only those who know they're lost experience the joy of being found.

An Overdue Apology to Acquiescers

I don't know what it's like to be a back-row sitter, slip-in-and-outer, stayer-under-the-radar. As your sister in Christ, I ought to know. We are, after all, one flock with one Shepherd.

I was so busy seeking attention that I didn't notice you. I'm sorry for how my self-absorption hurt you.

I was so focused on keeping up appearances that I was unapproachable. I'm sorry for how my arrogance hurt you.

I made you feel alone, certain you were the only one struggling while everyone else had it all together. I'm sorry for how my aloofness hurt you.

I pretended to listen while looking past you for the person I wanted to impress. I'm sorry for how my rudeness hurt you.

I paid attention to how others were reacting to me instead of investing in you. I'm sorry for how my pride hurt you.

I made you feel condemned, convinced that you could neither be yourself nor be loved. I'm sorry for how my judgment hurt you.

I own my actions and inactions. I was wrong. The 99 Club was pretend; your hurt was real. I pray that by God's grace, we will heal.

Together.

What Happens When You're Real

It's such a relief to stop impressing people and start expressing yourself. To quit acquiescing and commit to engaging.

Something extraordinary happens when you celebrate your membership in The One Club. When you stop impressing people and start expressing yourself, you develop humility.

Not the false humility of shapeshifting for others, which is pride in disguise, or of hiding from others, which is the strategy of shame. But a deep humility, demonstrated daily through gratitude and authenticity. You realize that what "be yourself" really means is sharing your rescue story and showing your scars.

As Amy says, "People don't need my perfection; they need God's power."

Sure, some people will sit back, cross their arms across their chest, shake their head, and think, *What can you possibly teach me?*

My classmates and I thought this about our algebra teacher when he told us he'd been a C student. But thirty years later, when hundreds of us showed up for Mr. B's memorial service, we all said the same things about him.

He always remembered how hard learning can be, so we knew that he knew how we felt when we got lost. He never gave up on us and was always exuberant when we finally "got it."

Our failures never fazed him. In fact, the classes I took from Mr. B are among the few precious times when I felt unafraid to fail. He made it safe to fail; thus, he made it safe to learn. In his presence, I could be myself—my real, messy, unimpressive, in-need-of-rescue, beloved self.

We can't yank anyone out of The 99 Club any more than we can force anyone out of hiding.

But by being yourself—your real, messy, unimpressive, acquiescing, in-need-of-rescue, beloved self—you can woo others toward The One Club with the life-changing truth that has forever transformed you: *You can be yourself and be loved—because you are beloved by God.*

 *now breathe*

Print and post this as a constant reminder:
I can be myself and be loved—because I am beloved by God.

(You'll find a lovely PDF, as well as cell phone and computer wall-paper images, at ExhaleBook.com.)

LOVE WHO YOU ARE:

You ARE the one Jesus seeks.

Part Two Quick Reference Guide to
Love Who You ARE

You ARE a limited edition of one.
You ARE a woman with a story linked to His.
You ARE gifted with God-given strengths.
You ARE beautifully quirky.
You ARE essential to the body of Christ.
You ARE a woman with a current calling.
You ARE the one Jesus seeks.

Old Mindset . . .	*New Mindset . . .*
So many people hold such authority over me.	God is the one true Authority in my life.
Difficult circumstances disqualify me.	God uses my trials to train me.
I must focus on overcoming my weaknesses.	God multiplies my meager into His much.
My uncommon gifts make me unwelcome.	God transforms my quirks into perks.
I'm desperate to belong.	We belong to God, so we belong together.
I'm uncertain about my calling.	Jesus calls me close and then sends me out.
I can be myself, or I can be loved.	I can be myself because I am beloved by God.

Part Three

LIVE YOUR ONE LIFE WELL

Whew! This has been quite the journey, hasn't it?

Losing who you're not isn't for the weak of heart. And loving who you are may take more courage still.

If you've been truly hiking the mountain of change with us, you may feel tired and stretched beyond what you ever thought you could do. Which is a really good place to be, since all that requires dependence on God!

Well, we're almost at the destination that we started at the beginning of this book, and there's some good news.

Although losing who you're not is an exhale that requires painful repentance . . .

And loving who you are necessitates trusting your Creator without reservation . . .

Living your one life well is a gasp of delight!

You heard it right. The bumpy roads of this adventure to the fullest God-given life are behind you. Smoother roads are ahead. Pathways of joy are right in front of you.

We can't promise that you won't ever be worn-out again, and we wouldn't dare tell you that life's going to be perfect. But we can guarantee that the result of all your labor—losing who you're not, loving who you are, and living your one life well—will be a happy tired instead of a running-on-empty tired.

Here we go!

Forge on to the end, brave reader. Forge on.

fifteen

Live in Animation: You're Meant to Be Fully Alive

Amy

When Mrs. Warren, my third-grade teacher, hovered over me to check my work or answer questions, all was right with the world. My eight-year-old heart basked in her presence. From the bottom of her color-coordinated espadrilles to the top of her Dorothy Hamill haircut, my teacher was divine. She looked like a teacher. She acted like a teacher. She even had the perfectly perfumed *smell* of a teacher, and I adored her.

Every lesson Mrs. Warren taught was creative and engaged my mind. She sang and strummed along on the autoharp, which was way hippy-cool. And one Friday a month was Freaky Friday—goody, oh boy, hip hip hooray!—when we did string art, skits, and other third-grade delights. My teacher was entirely wonderful, and I wanted to be just like her.

Mrs. Warren set me on a path that continued for decades. She released seeds of love for learning, a passion for teaching, and dedication to children that increased steadily.

My desire to become a teacher grew like a plant.

Roots fascinated with the way little minds worked plunged deep.

Helping with child care at church (until my parents insisted on periodic attendance in the service) was a stem pushing upward.

Babysitting leaves sprung out as I strove to be loved by neighborhood parents and children alike.

Buds emerged when I student-taught in college, followed by full-blown blooms in my classroom years.

My teaching bouquet graced elementary and adult-education classes, but they all started with a seed. Seeds Mrs. Warren launched into the wind of her third-grade classroom landed, rooted, and grew in my little-girl heart.

Gardening with Jesus

On the morning the first spring sun rises warm, dispelling the chill of a short North Carolina winter, my fingers start to itch. They long to dip into the soil outside, planting the flowers that will bloom through the long summer and fall seasons. I can't wait to get outdoors, dig some holes, and plant the seeds that will spring up tall and later colorful.

I start out with vim and some vigor to spare, but come midsummer, my zeal wanes. Last weekend on a sultry Saturday morning, I dragged myself outside to do weeding duties. Plants with names like *crabgrass* and *nutsedge* have taken over, and those seeds that I *didn't* plant are smothering the lovely annuals and perennials that bear the flowers I crave.

I plunge a long, sharp tool into the soil to loosen the weeds' root systems, and then I give them a firm yank, shaking the dirt back into the bed to nourish the plants that belong there before I toss the now half-dead weed into my wheelbarrow.

Almost instantly, the black-eyed Susans, the coneflowers, the daisies, and the zinnias look fresher. Perkier. And I know that freeing them up will soon lead to more delightful blooms.

I'm not exactly agrarian, but I do adore gardening. When Jesus talks about soil and seeds, plants and fruit, vines and branches, He's speaking a language that I love and that many of us understand. Even if you've never planted a field, maybe you've picked strawberries on a farm, apples from an orchard, or a pumpkin from a patch. You may not have plowed a straight furrow, but you may have raked a rut into the soil, dropping tiny seeds as you go. You may not have run a harvester through acres of grain, but you've picked wildflowers from the roadside or a stray dandelion from your lawn. If you haven't done any of these, maybe you've picked up a bouquet at the grocery store? We're creations who live from the fruit of the vine, so we grasp the Creator's stories of The Vine.

Of all the gospel writers, Mark capitalized best on Jesus's seed stories by stringing them together like a beaded necklace.

Mark's gospel contains three well-known parables that Jesus told, and when we look at them together, we see a progression that gives us steps into God's garden, His big story that runs from Genesis through Revelation.

God Is the Sower

In the scene described in Mark 4:1–8, Jesus is by the lake teaching, with a large crowd around Him, and He tells the famous story of the sower. A farmer scatters seed, but the seeds have different endings depending on the soil on which they fall. Some seeds are eaten by birds. Some grow quickly but then wither for lack of rich soil and a scorching sun. Other seeds grow but are runts because of thorns. But one set of seeds grows strong, producing an abundant crop because of the good soil where they landed.

In my imagination, I weave through the crowd, observing His listeners. There are many reactions.

Some are soothed to sleep by the sound of Jesus's storytelling voice and the waves lapping on the shore.

Others probably listen with an ear to be entertained. What a great afternoon it is to listen to a story! So much better than another day at home with nothing to do.

Some people's minds wander as the day lengthens. *I've got so much to do*, they think. And their mental lists grow while Jesus's voice fills the background of their thoughts.

But for a few, a very few, they hear the truth underneath the words, and their hearts respond.

In the original crowd of hearers, surely there is an instant manifestation of the truths Jesus is illustrating. Every kind of soil is represented, and the seeds of truth that Jesus sends out in His story land on every variety of heart-soil.

And I wonder, if I had been in the crowd, what would my response to the Seed Sender be?

A Crowd of Thorn-Choked Seeds

I'm pierced when I consider my heart's soil, because I know the answer. The majority of my life, my heart has been the thorny soil. The seed of truth landed and took root. Initially there was vibrant growth, but then my patch of soil became overgrown by worry, to-do lists, and the desire to please others.

Truthfully, until I slowed down to study for this chapter, I've never recognized myself as thorny. Surely I'm good soil because my faith is still alive. My relationship with Jesus has lasted for four decades now, so I'm good. Or am I?

An additional realization hit when I reached Mark 4:18–19 (ESV), where Jesus says, "And others are the ones sown among thorns. They are those who hear the word, but the cares of the world and the deceitfulness of riches and the desires for other things enter in and choke the word, and it proves unfruitful."

Oh . . . the seeds among the thorns weren't *dead*. They had sprung to life but were barely surviving. The seeds choked by the thorns were alive. They just weren't *fruitful*.

Ouch. Cares of the world? Check. Desires for other things? (Hello, approval-seeking!) Check.

How do Jesus-loving women like me let thorns thrive, anyway? When the thorns burst from the soil, they aren't viny, choky, or thorny yet. They're just this little set of innocent-looking leaves. That's true in our lives, too. The thorny issues that start to choke us later—unrealistic expectations, out-of-control schedules, negative labels, and the ilk—start small and innocuous. It's only later that their destructive nature becomes apparent, and then it feels too late.

It's painful to even write these things, but there's hope. Jesus doesn't scatter His Word and then leave us. He doesn't abandon us to the thorns. In John 15:1–5, 11 (ESV), Jesus shows us how to regain the fruitfulness for which we're made:

> I am the true vine, and my Father is the vinedresser. Every branch in me that does not bear fruit he takes away, and every branch that does bear fruit he prunes, that it may bear more fruit. Already you are clean because of the word that I have spoken to you. Abide in me, and I in you. As the branch cannot bear fruit by itself, unless it abides in the vine, neither can you, unless you abide in me. I am the vine; you are the branches. Whoever abides in me and I in him, he it is that bears much fruit, for apart from me you can do nothing. . . . These things I have spoken to you, that my joy may be in you, and that your joy may be full.

When God created us, He himself planted seeds of purpose in us, and we'll never be fully satisfied until we're fully animated, brought to life, and full of the Spirit. Our level of animation is revealed in our fruitfulness. Thorns smother the seed. But allowing God to prune away the worries we bear and the approval from others that we crave releases the original potential for growth and fruitfulness woven into the DNA of the seed. Just as I work in my planting bed to remove the weeds that diminish the beauty woven into the fiber of my flowers, God faithfully removes the thorns from our lives when we invite Him.

We Are Sowers

In Mark 4:26–29, we find a parable that is only retold in this gospel:

> He also said, "This is what the kingdom of God is like. A man scatters seed on the ground. Night and day, whether he sleeps or gets up, the seed sprouts and grows, though he does not know how. All by itself the soil produces grain—first the stalk, then the head, then the full kernel in the head. As soon as the grain is ripe, he puts the sickle to it, because the harvest has come."

In this story, Jesus shifts the pictures a bit. Here, *we* are the sower! Bask in that for just a moment. God is the Sower, but He also invites us to join Him so we're part of His life-giving process.

What an incredible gift. When we grow and are fruitful, suddenly we burst forth with new seeds. God gives us the seeds of His Word. He gives us gifts. He gives us a commission, and then He purposes us to be His seed senders. That divine purpose is customized for each one of His unique girls.

Mrs. Warren sent the seeds of teaching into my life.

My mom sent seeds of mothering and homemaking into my earliest memories.

Layne, an early mentor, sent the seeds of a Jesus-centered life into my teenaged heart.

Jean, a college leader, sent the seeds of deep Bible study into me as a young woman.

Mona, a ministry partner, sent the seeds of wise words into my leadership days.

Thinking of the seeds sent by dozens of women that impacted me makes me teary-eyed. Look in your hands. What seeds do you have to send?

Career building, adoption, leadership, mothering, Bible teaching, goal setting, encouragement . . .

The list of seeds to be sent is endless because our God is infinitely creative in us. As my wise friend Kendra said, "We're not required to send specific seeds in specific ways, thinking that we've got God's plans for our lives all nailed down. When we're exhaling and not busy hyperventilating, we're *always* sending seeds."

Kendra followed with another picture that made all the lightbulbs in my head explode. She said, "Have you ever seen a small child trying to blow dandelion seeds? They have the passion, but it's all hard blowing and no movement. Just like the toddler, we can have passion—boy, we *want* to blow those seeds all over the place—but unless it's a steady, calm, Spirit-led exhale, we're not sending seed, we're just spitting in the wind."

Oh. My. I see myself so well in that toddler trying to blow a dandelion! For example, I remember the day I looked in the mirror and told myself, "If you don't publish a book by the time you're fifty, Amy, you're finished."

I had a seed, some words and messages, in my heart, so I thought that I had to accomplish a goal in a set way and certain timing. This is the way I've thought for years. My work/purpose/calling was either the next thing in front of me or a self-determined end goal with a self-generated time line.

"What if I haven't taught you what you need to write until you're eighty, Amy?" Jesus whispered to my heart. "Will you still write then?"

God has given us seeds, but we don't know how they grow. He alone has the power and the timing.

Exhale. Send. Repeat. Again, what seeds do you hold in your hand?

Fruit Is the Point

Those seeds are meant to be sent out. They're designed to fly, propelled on the wind of God's Spirit until they land, grow, and produce fruit. We seed senders may not understand how our seeds grow, but it's a delight to watch them burst forth. "All by itself the soil produces grain—first the stalk, then the head, then the full kernel in the head" (Mark 4:28).

Fruitfulness is the pinnacle of every life. The Sower scatters seeds, and the ones landing in good soil produce "a crop, some multiplying thirty, some sixty, some a hundred times" (v. 8). A man sows and a harvest comes (v. 29). A miniscule seed is planted and a humongous plant grows (v. 32).

Do you feel the sense of longing rising up, wanting to be God's partner not just in paltry produce but in abundance? That longing in us comes from Him so that we'll abide in Him, letting Him tend us until a bumper crop appears. Any other way of life leaves us listless, unsatisfied, and frustrated. Discontent with less than we were made for keeps us up in the middle of the night. To find true fulfillment, we live the life of a seed sender, watching the divine Grower and Harvester reap crops through us.

The Kingdom Grows

In the final parable of Matthew 4, Jesus compares the kingdom of God to a mustard seed. This seed starts tiny but grows into the largest of all garden plants, and it's the shelter for those who flock to it.

These parables are pictures of the steps we need to take, friends.

God sows. → *We sow.* → *The kingdom grows.*

You know me well by now. I'm Action Amy (not a compliment—remember?), a flawed mom and wife, a woman who slogs through repeated failures, and a daughter of the King who has allowed the thorns to grow up. Now that you know me, can I confess to you?

This chapter is where I wanted the book to start. I wanted to urge you to stop spending your life and to start investing it. I wanted to inspire you to action, assuring you that you can never pour out more than you'll get. I wanted you to find your call and confirm your gifts so that you can *use* them. My desire was that you would be fully animated and abundantly fruitful.

Thankfully, our gentle friend Cheri intervened for your sake. She reminded me that we reforming perfectionists and people-pleasers, we who want all the people to be happy all the time, would be completely overwhelmed by a book like that. She cautioned me that a message that strong would set you (and *us!*) up for failure. She pointed out that women like you, who are wired just like the two of us, would simply add lessons about your calling and work to the list that you already have. Cheri rightly encouraged me that we needed a process before the call to action.

Then, Cheri spelled out the steps in this book. Lose who you're not . . . by identifying and pulling the weeds that have been choking out your fruit. Love who you are . . . by seeing yourself as a flawed but beautifully gifted woman with hands full of flowers that are ready to burst forth into seeds. Then, and only then, you'd be able to live your one life well. Only after the first two steps would we be able to see this:

Live your one life well = Live your one life as a seed sender

Some things never change, and God used Cheri to temper Action Amy, reminding her of some truths that needed to come first.

But now is the time!

All the work you did since the beginning of the book . . .

- embracing failure as a part of change
- letting others assume their responsibilities as you shoulder your own
- peeling off your old labels and discarding them
- finding joy in the woman God created you to be
- leveraging your redeemed flaws and quirks
- discovering your callings and gifts

All that work is valuable because *you* are valuable, but it's not the end.

You don't do that work so that you can simply stop trying to be everything for everyone . . . although Cheri and I dream that you have.

It isn't just so that you can feel better about yourself . . . although we pray that you do.

It isn't only so that you can have more margin in your schedule . . . although we hope that you might.

It isn't even so that you give mental assent to your valuable calling.

Cheri and I want you to lose who you're not so that the weeds that have been choking out your fruitfulness are uprooted and thrown into the compost pile. We want you to love who you are so that you see yourself worthy in God's eyes.

Ultimately, though, we want to inspire you to become something. Not something other than who you are, but fully animated into who you've always been designed to be. We want you to be a seed sender.

Working on ourselves is a process needed to move into God's big story. He calls us to know and animate our callings, not simply for self-fulfillment but to build His kingdom. His kingdom isn't limited to the walls of churches. It's in workplaces and homes. Neighborhoods and cities. Hospital rooms and domestic violence shelters. God's kingdom is being built wherever His seed-sending people are.

This is the part where my throat clenches with emotion and my eyes fill with tears of longing. This is the moment when I want you and me to be consumed with the life created for us. I want us to be swallowed up with the desire to be a seed sender. The good news? Being a seed sender both powerfully glorifies God and deeply fulfills us.

I picture us as a field of women standing almost shoulder to shoulder with flowers filling our hands. The flowers are in full bloom, bursting with seeds. Suddenly the wind starts to blow. It's gentle at first, but just as God always does, the wind of the Spirit grows in power. As the wind strengthens, we lift our hands as one, offering our flowers to its force, and the seeds begin to blow, and we lift our faces to watch.

We don't know where the seeds are going exactly. We're just the seed senders. We're not the Seed Grower, but we know Him. So we trust and wait with expectation, dreaming of a field on the horizon, until the fruit appears, and then, raising our arms with joy, we rejoice together.

✳ *now breathe*

Holding your hands open and cupped before you, imagine and name the seeds you hold. Now close your eyes, and ask the divine Gardener to activate you, turning you into a fruitful seed sender.

LIVE YOUR ONE LIFE WELL:

Live life as a vibrant seed sender.

sixteen

Live Open to Redirection:
A New Dream Can Give You New Life

Cheri

"What should I do next?"

It's the question on my mind every morning when I wake up. I want to know what I'm supposed to do today. This morning. Right now.

I love a good plan.

I create dream boards and goal charts and checklists and time lines. And then I plow right through them. Once I've set my intention for sowing and growing, I want fast fruits.

But God's been teaching me that following Him means remaining open to His direction . . . and redirection.

Sometimes He'll start a new dream in my heart. Sometimes He'll stop me from executing my plans. And sometimes He'll swap out an old goal for a new one.

Inevitably, the answer to "What should I do next?" is Start, Stop, or Swap.

Start

Buying the basil plant was an act of irresponsible optimism.

My home is where plants go to die.

But my son wanted to make pesto, and all the "fresh basil" in the produce aisle was turning black. I was texting, "Sorry, son, there is no fresh basil, not even for ready money!" when I noticed a row of live basil plants in the floral section.

Score!

Even if it only survived long enough for one batch of pesto, it was well worth $2.99!

Somehow, though, The Little Basil Plant That Could hung on, day in and day out. A full week went by without any sign of brown leaves. (I could practically hear him chanting, "I think I can! I think I can! I think I can!")

Eager to be a good plant mom, I read up on the care and feeding of basil plants. Since they love sun, I started putting Basil outside each afternoon.

Too late, I learned about whiteflies.

Basil put up a good fight, but the damage was too great. All his leaves fell off and his green stems turned brown. Defeated, I left my latest gardening failure out on the back porch.

Months passed.

Then one day, I noticed something unexpected: *signs of life!* Six tiny green leaves sprouting at the base of one brown stem.

I cut down the dead stems, brought Basil inside, watered him, and set him in a window with afternoon sun. A few weeks later, four of the leaves were the size of my thumbnail, and two were the size of my palm, ready for harvest.

My first crop!

During this same month, I received an unexpected rejection for a project I'd been so sure God was giving the "go." Specifically, a book proposal I'd been working on for several years. Month after month, it got better and better. But ultimately, my own "whiteflies"—a host of seemingly small issues—brought it crashing down in the form of a very pointed rejection letter.

I threw myself a humdinger of a pity party over my defeat. Phrases like *"After all the time, effort, and money I've spent on . . . ,"* *"This is all I have to show for twenty-five years of . . .,"* *"I should just quit once and for . . ."* had been swirling through my mind, day and night.

But tending to Basil made me wonder: *What if my dream isn't dead? What if, like my feisty little plant, it's simply dormant? What if there's still life in it?*

I started thinking about how I could cut back the deadwood from my dream. Perhaps even transplant it into a different container.

And sure enough—my dream began to sprout anew.

Stop

Basil had grown such big beautiful leaves. But I was feeling so successful, I didn't want to remove them. I wanted to keep watching them grow bigger and bigger. So I kept telling myself, "I'll cut off the biggest leaves tomorrow." When tomorrow came, I told myself, "I'll cut off the biggest leaves tomorrow." For ten tomorrows.

Finally, I had to face the truth: Basil had stopped growing.

I pulled out my kitchen shears, took a deep breath, and started cutting leaves. When I was done, poor Basil looked so forlorn. I pitied him. *Just look at that one sad little leaf all alone at the top.*

And me? *I look like such a failure as a windowsill farmer.*

But then I wondered. *What if one leaf is just right for right now?*

Evidently, it was. Ten days later, Basil sported dozens of leaves. His largest new leaves were bigger than any of those I'd been so reluctant to harvest less than two weeks prior.

I'd heard it before, but I didn't believe it until I saw it with my own eyes: Pruning increases productivity.

Stopping for a while doesn't mean stopping forever.

Every time I've read the parable of the talents, I've felt sorry for the poor servant who got one measly talent:

For it will be like a man going on a journey, who called his servants and entrusted to them his property. To one he gave five talents, to another two, to another one, to each according to his ability. Then he went away. He who had received the five talents went at once and traded with them, and he made five talents more. So also he who had the two talents made two talents more. But he who had received the one talent went and dug in the ground and hid his master's money.

Matthew 25:14–18 ESV

I understand burying the booby prize. But recently it occurred to me: *What if one talent isn't a lesser gift?*

For so many years, I strove to make it clear to the watching world: *I am a five-talent servant, thank you very much.*

Until I discovered that I'm not. I'm an HSP—a Highly Sensitive Person—with a smaller-than-average capacity for productivity. Which I'm learning to accept. Begrudgingly, that is. Because I can do basic math: Five is greater than one, so five is obviously *better* than one.

But what if one talent isn't a lesser gift? What if one talent is just right for right now?

What if the Master knows His servants so well that He knows when one talent is the perfect fit? For our unique personalities? Our past experiences? Our current season of life?

Sometimes, when we can't do All The Things, we pout and do No Thing. Or we overwhelm ourselves trying to do All The Things because we can't face the shame of being a one-talent servant.

But what if one talent isn't a lesser gift? What if one talent is just right for right now?

What if one talent is the gift of focus?

What if it's high time to cut back on All The Things we're over-attempting, but we're way too fond of showing off our leaves? What if we're shrinking back from the pruning shears right when we need to welcome the chance for new growth?

As it turns out, letting go of a dead dream can be an enormous relief.

I've loved writing ever since my mother "published" my first book when I was just two years old. But the process of writing book proposals was utterly draining for me. I hadn't realized how much it took out of me until I shelved all the ideas I'd been working on for the previous three years.

I felt lighter. Freer. Eager to write just for fun. I had no idea how much dead weight I'd been carrying until I set it down.

None of this comes as a surprise, especially not after Amy walked us through John 15:1–5 in the previous chapter. "I am the true vine, and my Father is the gardener. He cuts off every branch in me that bears no fruit, *while every branch that does bear fruit he prunes so that it will be even more fruitful*" (vv. 1–2, emphasis added).

How quickly, in our ongoing battles with comparison, we forget that God's math is so different from ours. We strive for bigger and better. And then we cling to All The Things, terrified of losing what we have. Letting go feels like too great a risk.

So we live unpruned, even wildly overgrown, lives. All our time and energy devoted to maintaining. Surviving, not thriving.

Like my basil plant, you and I can hold on to what we have now, or we can grow and flourish.

We can't do both.

God longs to give you all that He has in store for you next— "infinitely more than we might ask or think" (Ephesians 3:20 NLT).

He needs to subtract so there's space for Him to multiply.

Do you sense Him inviting you to stop some specific dreams, setting them aside for a season or perhaps forever? If so, remember:

One talent isn't a lesser gift.

One talent is just right for right now.

One talent is the gift of focus.

Swap

I learned my one-talent servant lessons:

1. Pruning increases productivity.
2. One leaf—like one talent—is enough.
3. Focus is a gift.

So focus I did. I poured all my windowsill gardening energies on one goal: *Keep Basil alive.* This was the ultimate test. Faithfully, I watered and pruned, watered and pruned.

One day, to my delight, I discovered that Basil was sprouting an abundance of tiny new leaves, all bunched together. *Look at me and my bad self, keeping Basil alive and helping him thrive!*

I felt downright smug. *I'm growing a green thumb!*

But as the days passed, the tiny new leaves didn't get any bigger, no matter how much I watered Basil. Finally I realized: *These aren't leaves; they're flowers.*

Frantically, I Googled "my basil plant is flowering" and discovered—to my horror—that basil plants normally produce a few cycles of leaves, flower, **and then they die.**

My immediate response was panic: *No! Basil can't die! I promised to keep him alive!!*

Followed by: *Wait, basil plants are supposed to die? So if . . . when . . . Basil dies, it won't mean that I'm a failure?*

And then: *What if this is true of all our dreams? What if no one dream is meant to be the "ultimate"? What if each dream is supposed to seed the next?*

Embracing a new dream can be revitalizing and even revolutionary.

When I swapped my dream of writing books with starting a podcast, I felt excited but apprehensive. Part of me worried that I was copping out. Like, I couldn't make it as an author, so I was settling for the next best thing.

But within a few episodes, we were "having more fun than should be allowed" (to quote Amy). We thrived on collaboration. We soaked up wisdom from other authors. We experienced God's transforming power through women's authentic stories and voices. And we were amazed as our little audience of listeners grew week after week!

Podcasting has caused mindset changes in me that I now know, in retrospect, I desperately needed. And podcasting was the only way I could have learned what I've learned, grown as I've grown.

If you're holding on to a dream that's nearing (or at) end-of-life, open yourself up to how and where God is leading you. As you go through the swap process:

1. **Monitor your dread.** Don't let it ratchet so high that you're paralyzed by misery. When you let a dead dream go, dread lets go of you.

2. **Monitor the coexistence of your dying dream and new dream.** Don't steal what rightfully belongs to the new dream to extend the life of the old. At some point, you must let go.

3. **Monitor your relief level as you let the dead dream go.** Don't let guilt and shame step in. It's okay to be glad it's finally over.

4. **Monitor your renewed energy.** Don't keep it under wraps. Show respect for all that the dead dream taught you by diving fully into the new.

Remember: No one dream is meant to be the "ultimate" dream. Each dream is supposed to seed your next.

Discerning Tier 1, Tier 2, and Tier 3 Goals

I picked the wrong dream in the first place.

Reading Angela Duckworth's book *Grit: The Power of Passion and Perseverance*, I realized where I'd gone wrong with my basil plant, with my book publishing goals, and dozens of other dreams throughout my life.

Early on, she explores a concept she calls "the hierarchy of goals." A simplified visual looks like this:

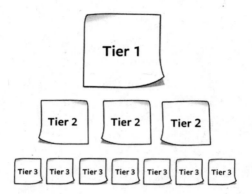

Duckworth discusses the importance of ordering our goals appropriately:

Grit is about holding the same top-level [Tier 1] goal for a very long time. . . . In very gritty people, most mid-level [Tier 2] and low-level [Tier 3] goals are, in some way or another, related to that ultimate goal. . . . You need one internal compass—not two, three, four, or five.[1]

After reading this, and mulling over the diagram, I emailed Amy:

For a decade, people like you have been telling me, "It's about the message not the medium." But that simply doesn't sink in to a girl who has dreamed of writing books since she was two years old.

NOW, after devoting YEARS to numerous book proposals that aren't going anywhere—I finally get it.

I mistakenly thought that "Get a Book Deal" was my Tier 1 goal. And so I kept changing topics hoping to hit on a topic—ANY TOPIC!— a publisher might print.

1. Angela Duckworth, *Grit: The Power of Passion and Perseverance* (New York: Scribner, 2016), 64, 67.

But books are Tier 2 goals at best. Honestly, they may well be Tier 3 goals at this point in my life—worth a shot but NOT years of my life.

My message, all the way back to when my mother took me to hear Florence Littauer, has always been around personality and temperament, which includes being an HSP [Highly Sensitive Person]. And about what can go wrong when we don't know and accept our God-given selves: perfectionism and people-pleasing.

Equipping women so they can be set free to receive God's love has always been my true Tier 1 goal.

I'll bet my life would feel a lot less stressful—and a lot more rewarding!—if my goal hierarchy looked like this:

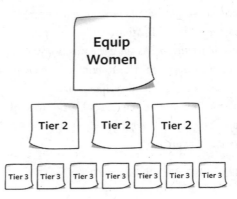

Anyhow, that's my a-HA for the day.

A couple of hours later, after more reflection, I fired off this follow-up:

Here's my next a-HA:

You know how for some gals (like me), rejection of their book proposal = MY LIFE IS OVER?

Well, if the book proposal was, in fact, their ONE TIER 1 GOAL and it was blocked, then of COURSE their life is over! They're not being drama queens . . . they're being honest!

Now, the question is: How do we choose Tier 1 and Tier 2 goals that NOBODY CAN BLOCK? That may end up detoured but never dead-ended?

Any goal that can be blocked or become a dead end, it seems to me now, should never be given anything other than Tier 3 goal status. Nice if it happens, but there's always Plans B, C, D, E, . . . ZZ if it doesn't happen.

All fabulous in theory, of course. Now, to try to live it out . . . !!

When we pick Tier 1 goals that aren't sustainable, we doom ourselves to disappointment. Discouragement. Even despair.

For me, "Keep Basil Alive" wasn't a worthy Tier 1 goal. There were too many factors beyond my control: temperature, sunshine, whiteflies, and the fact that basil plants don't live forever. So I've changed my basil Tier 1 goal to "Use Fresh Basil," which I can always do.

As soon as I harvested Basil's last leaves, he went into the compost heap. By now, I've bought dozens of replacements since that original basil plant. I don't need to keep any one particular basil plant alive. As long as a basil plant is thriving in my windowsill at any given time, it's all good.

When I downgraded "Get a Book Contract" to a Tier 3 goal, I believed that I'd never write another book. A year later, when Amy told me she needed to talk with me about something important, I feared she was going to tell me she was quitting the podcast. Instead, she asked me to pray about co-authoring a book with her. This book.

But as grateful as I am for the privilege of writing another book, "Get a Book Contract" is no longer my holy grail. I fulfill God's Tier 1 call to "Equip Women" through Tier 2 and Tier 3 methods as varied as listening to my friends, mentoring teens, leading the *Grit 'n' Grace* intern team, and working on my graduate degree.

What about you: What is your basil? Your book deal?

What dream have you clung to, regardless of how damaging it's become to you and those you love? What dream have you elevated to Tier 1 goal status but you cannot sustain? What dream has hit dead ends because other people have blocked it?

Ephesians 2:10 (ESV) says that we are "created in Christ Jesus for good works." *Works*, plural. No one work is meant to be our ultimate dream. In fact, our ultimate dream is not earthly, but eternal. And no dream is ever meant to fulfill us; only the Dream Giver offers true fulfillment.

If you're mourning the loss of a dream, by all means grieve. But as you do, keep your eyes open. While releasing what's no longer yours, watch for signs of new life.

Be a front-row witness as hope is reborn.

Get out a stack of Post-it Notes, a Sharpie (or a pencil with an eraser if it makes it easier for you to make competent mistakes), and a foam core board (or empty table or window or wall). Pray-cess your own Tier 1 goals, Tier 2 goals, and Tier 3 goals. As you do, ask yourself the questions below:

1. **Start**: What dreams, goals, or plans have I started? Which ones have flourished? Why? Which ones have died? Why?

2. **Stop**: What dreams, goals, or plans have I had to stop? Why? What do I sense God calling me to stop now, even if I don't know why?

3. **Swap**: What dreams, goals, or plans have I swapped? How did I feel at the time? What do I see now in hindsight?

(You'll find detailed instructions and a helpful template at Exhale-Book.com.)

LIVE YOUR ONE LIFE WELL:

Live open to God's direction and redirection.

seventeen

Live in Restoration:
Delight Is Your Birthright

Cheri

According to my parents, I had a silly habit when I was a little girl.

During family gatherings, I'd march from person to person, declaring and pointing, "I love DADDY! And I love MOMMY! And I love JOHNNY! And I love G'ama! And I love G'ampa!"

When I got done proclaiming my love for all the people in the room, I'd walk to the center of the room, throw my arms around myself, and make one last announcement.

"And most of all, I love ME!"

I have no memories of this gutsy girl who knew she was lovable and embraced herself with such gusto. I wish I did.

The girl I do remember started almost every high school journal entry with, "Whew! I survived!" And then sketched her jam-packed schedule and detailed to-do lists for making it through The Next Big Thing, like exam week or drama performance or the Christmas program—or all three at the same time. Yes, I was an overattempter even way back when.

"I'm starting a diet today" shows up halfway through my high school journals. Followed by calorie counts and increasingly rigid food plans interspersed between my calendars and checklists.

Initially, I just wanted to lose three pounds. But reaching that goal felt so satisfying, I decided to lose three more. Followed by three more. As my body shrank in size, so did my focus. Losing weight became my primary source of comfort.

Sure, I was constantly hungry. But hunger made me happy because it signaled that I was in control of at least one aspect of my life: what I did or didn't eat. The greater my sense of control, the less stress, worry, and anxiety I felt, which was a welcome relief.

Especially at 2:37 a.m.

"He Delighted in Me"

I lost so much weight during high school that the day after graduation, my parents checked me into the eating disorder unit of a Southern California neuropsychiatric hospital.

"Anorexia nervosa is not just extreme dieting," the doctor told them during admission. "Anorexia nervosa is attempting to commit suicide, slowly."

I rolled my eyes and silently contradicted him: *I'm not trying to kill myself. I just need to lose three more pounds.*

A couple of weeks into my hospitalization, we had a difficult family counseling session. My counselor urged me to be open, honest, and vulnerable with my parents. But sharing my feelings was the last thing on earth I was going to do. *We are a family of thinkers, not feelers, thank you kindly.* I set my jaw and vowed to maintain control if it killed me.

After the session, I tossed and turned into the wee hours of the night. Finally, I opened my Bible, hoping to read myself to sleep. In Psalm 18:4–19, I read:

> The cords of death entangled me;
>> the torrents of destruction overwhelmed me.

This is me! My doctor is right; I am dying. I swallowed, my throat dry.

The cords of the grave coiled around me;
  the snares of death confronted me.

My heart pounded in my ears. *I don't want to die!*

In my distress I called to the Lord;
  I cried to my God for help. . . .

But I'm buried so far under. I gasped for breath.

He reached down from on high and took hold of me;
  he drew me out of deep waters.

I rocked back and forth. *I don't know how to get out.*

He rescued me from my powerful enemy,
  from my foes, who were too strong for me.

But I know I want to . . . live.

They confronted me in my day of disaster,
  but the Lord was my support.

I want to live. My own life, for once.

He brought me out into a spacious place;
  he rescued me because he delighted in me.

***God** delights in me.*
*God **delights** in me?*
*God delights in **me**!*

As I clasped my hands to my chest and inhaled deeply, the gutsy little girl in me began to giggle. An unbidden smile brought a sparkle to my eyes.

Maybe . . . maybe I can learn to delight in myself the way God delights in me?

"A Spacious Place"

God rescued me that night in the eating disorder unit.

And then He invited me to stay with Him in "a spacious place"— *our* spacious place. I was grateful that He'd saved my life; I really and truly was. But I did not take Him up on His offer.

Rescue, yes. Refuge, no.

Instead I told Him, in action if not in word, "Thank you for rescuing me! I've got it from here. You can go take care of someone else now."

I figured that saving was God's job, living was mine.

So I rolled up my sleeves and got busy with self-improvement.

I went to the Christian bookstore, where I bought several different Bible translations and a stack of concordances. I set my alarm for quiet time every morning and wrote out my prayers longhand. I attended women's study groups and filled in every blank in my study guide.

I thought of this (and so much more) as "spiritual growth." It looked good. It felt good, or at least familiar. Because it was my high school schedules and to-do lists and journals and checklists all over again, just with brand-new Bibles instead of high school textbooks.

My attempts to transform myself escalated with each major milestone. Marriage led me to Barnes & Noble, children meant attending local moms groups, and teaching took me to conferences.

But no matter how many affirmations I taped to my mirror, how many items I added to my gratitude list, how many random acts of kindness I committed, I couldn't escape the weight. The air felt too heavy to breathe, and God felt so distant. I couldn't escape the nagging thoughts in the wee hours of the night: *There must be more to life than this! What am I doing wrong?*

What I was doing wasn't inherently wrong. My problem was why I did what I did. I sought control through man-made systems, when what I needed was to take refuge in my Savior.

"Woman, You Are Set Free"

Those of us who understand *rescue* but can't quite grasp *refuge* have much to learn from Jesus's healing of the woman who was bent over for eighteen years.

If you've read it in the King James Version, you're familiar with the words "Woman, thou art loosed!"—a phrase that's always made my heart quicken and the corners of my eyes sting, although I've only recently understood why.

> On a Sabbath Jesus was teaching in one of the synagogues, and a woman was there who had been crippled by a spirit for eighteen years. She was bent over and could not straighten up at all. When Jesus saw her, he called her forward and said to her, "Woman, you are set free from your infirmity." Then he put his hands on her, and immediately she straightened up and praised God.
>
> Indignant because Jesus had healed on the Sabbath, the synagogue leader said to the people, "There are six days for work. So come and be healed on those days, not on the Sabbath."
>
> The Lord answered him, "You hypocrites! Doesn't each of you on the Sabbath untie your ox or donkey from the stall and lead it out to give it water? Then should not this woman, a daughter of Abraham, whom Satan has kept bound for eighteen long years, be set free on the Sabbath day from what bound her?"
>
> When he said this, all his opponents were humiliated, but the people were delighted with all the wonderful things he was doing.
>
> Luke 13:10–17

Luke spells out this woman's condition in vivid detail. She was bent over. (*Oh, how sad.*) Could not straighten up. (*Oh, that's bad.*) At all. (*Wow, I get it now.*)

I know this woman. Although I've never been physically crippled, for eighteen years—eighteen *long* years!—I carried the burden of being the good girl, the family hero, the keeper of too many secrets.

Jesus takes full initiative. He notices her. Invites her to come to Him. And then frees her from what's held her hostage.

He did the same for me that night in the hospital so many years ago. The heaviness I'd worked so hard to lose was lifted. In its place came a lightness that felt vaguely familiar and almost too good to be true.

Perhaps the woman feels this way, too, in the face of the irate synagogue leader. He ignores her, taking a passive-aggressive approach and lecturing the entire crowd about how they should come to be healed on business days, not the day of rest. The NASB says "get healed"—as if healing is a product that can be bought and sold.

This was how I once viewed healing. Perhaps you, too, have expected "one and done"? But Jesus offers so much more!

Here, Jesus begins a personal transformation on a relational day. But all the synagogue leader sees is a business transaction done the wrong way. What a missed opportunity to give glory to God for this miraculous healing! And such a sad distortion, defining the Sabbath according to what people should or should not do rather than by what God has done and is doing.

I know a thing or two about this kind of Sabbath shaming. I've doubled up under the weight of rigid rules and legalistic expectations. As a pastor's wife raising a pastor's kids, I've felt the hopelessness of facing unscalable expectations and the loneliness of hiding in solitary confinement. I've done time in a prison cell with ever-thickening walls built of thou-shalt-not bricks.

As Jesus evokes the tactile imagery of literal untying and unbinding, I think back to that night in the hospital when I read Psalm 18 for the first time:

> The cords of death entangled me. . . .
> The cords of the grave coiled around me;
>   the snares of death confronted me. . . .
> He brought me out into a spacious place.
>   he rescued me because he delighted in me.

Jesus's words, "Should not this woman, a daughter of Abraham, whom Satan has kept bound for eighteen long years, be set free on the

Sabbath day from what bound her?" are for us. Through this miracle, He showcases Sabbath as a sanctuary in time, built by God not for transaction but for transformation.

Jesus, my Rescuer, invites me to take refuge in Him.

I know how to receive rescue, but I've resisted refuge for so long—rescue, yes; refuge, no. But I need both. Taking refuge in God reunites me with the gutsy little girl who could say, "And most of all, I love ME!" Because that's who He created me to be.

And that's how He created us to live.

Refuge and Restoration

The "spacious place" of Psalm 18:19 isn't out there. You don't have to hunt to find refuge in God. Acts 17:28 tells us that "in him we live and move and have our being." You can take refuge in Him wherever you are because He is always right there with you in your day-to-day life. As the psalmist says so poetically:

> Where can I go from your Spirit?
> > Where can I flee from your presence?
> If I go up to the heavens, you are there;
> > if I make my bed in the depths, you are there.
> If I rise on the wings of the dawn,
> > if I settle on the far side of the sea,
> even there your hand will guide me,
> > your right hand will hold me fast.
>
> Psalm 139:7–10

Deep restoration happens in the spacious place where God delights in you and you in Him.

And oh, how we need deep restoration. For centuries, women have borne the stigma of first-to-sin. It was "the woman" who wandered, listened to the serpent, ate of the forbidden fruit, and gave it to her husband. Eve's to blame, and we are all daughters of Eve. So we suffer guilt by association. Carrying the burden of the fall, we have lived crippled for many long years: bent over, unable to straighten up at all.

When we take refuge, Jesus reminds us: "Woman, you are set free!" He dealt with the problem of sin at the cross, once and for all. The curse is broken; we are no longer condemned but redeemed!

Take the refuge God offers, and you'll live your one life well—in three distinct ways.

1. As you take refuge, you'll live YOUR one life well

Jesus's purpose is restoration, reuniting you with who He created you to be.

What happens in your heart when you watch a reunion scene? I still get teary just thinking about the old dog cresting the hill in *Homeward Bound*, limping toward his boy. I lose it at airports when separated lovers fall into a long-awaited embrace. And I am utterly undone by video compilations of soldiers returning home, their delighted children flinging themselves into waiting arms.

Our hearts beat to the rhythm of reunion.

And the most poignant reunion you will experience is not with a pet or husband or parent or child coming home. Your most healing homecoming is with your true self: that gutsy little girl who knows the world's problems were never her responsibility to solve.

So you can fling your arms around yourself and wholeheartedly declare, "And most of all, I love ME!" Which means nothing more or less than "I am delighted with who God has created me to be, with all God is doing in me and through me!"

2. As you take refuge, you'll live your ONE life well

Living your ONE and only life is such a relief.

It's the opposite of living hypothetical lives.

When you're in your spacious place, you're no longer chasing dozens of fear-fueled hypothetical lives, wondering why you feel so distant from God. When you take refuge, you walk through each day with Jesus, who is Immanuel: God with us. You hear and take to heart His words in Matthew 11:28–30 (MESSAGE):

> Are you tired? Worn out? Burned out on religion? Come to me. Get away with me and you'll recover your life. I'll show you how to take a real rest. Walk with me and work with me—watch how I do it. Learn the unforced rhythms of grace. I won't lay anything heavy or ill-fitting on you. Keep company with me and you'll learn to live freely and lightly.

With Jesus you can live just ONE life . . . and live it well.

3. As you take refuge, you'll live your one life WELL

Think of the word *well* with double meanings.

On the one hand, you want to be healed, saved, released from what has bound you. When Jesus asks, "Do you want to get well?" you want to say, "Yes!" and receive freedom.

On the other hand, you want to live with excellence. You want to take action in obedience. You want to hear God say, "Well done, my good and faithful servant!"

Get *well*.

Well done.

Noticing the Need with Your Name on It

She needs anyone but me.

Outwardly, I'm keeping my composure, but inside, I'm a turmoil of stunned heart and twisted stomach.

I walked into this retreat center kitchen for a quick sandwich, but the cook is sharing with me her story of gut-wrenching loss: the death of her twenty-seven-year-old daughter, just four months ago.

What do I say? I'm no good at comforting people. I'll just say the wrong thing. I have nothing to offer her. She needs anyone but me.

I thank her for the sandwich and head back to my room. On the way, I sense the Holy Spirit nudging me. *I could send her a copy of* Tear Soup.

Tear Soup is a book about processing loss I discovered earlier in the year, when a beloved teacher on our campus died suddenly, leaving the entire faculty and student body in shock and deep grief.

Order her a book? What a pitiful thing to do.

Afraid I'll chicken out, as I have so many times before, I pick up my pace to a run. Even as I point-and-click my way through the Amazon ordering process, I berate myself: *I should have prayed over her. Spoken encouragement over her. Why do I never have the right words when I need them?*

Throughout the next week, each time I think of Coleen, I feel shame. *What was I thinking? Ordering a book couldn't possibly be a call from God. She needed anyone but me.*

The next weekend, I return to the same retreat center for the second part of a two-part retreat. I want to avoid the cafeteria altogether, but as the speaker, I'm expected to eat with the women. Feeling like a foolish failure, I practice that apology speech I plan to deliver at the first opportunity.

But Coleen sneaks up on me Friday night. Envelops me in an all-encompassing hug, holding me like a long-lost friend. When she finally releases me, wiping tears from her smiling face, she holds out a long envelope. "Read it later," she says.

After the evening meeting, I return to my room. It's been thirty years since the night in the eating disorder unit when I read Psalm 18:19 for the very first time.

> He brought me out into a spacious place;
> he rescued me because he delighted in me.

I unfold Coleen's three-page typed letter, and my own tears begin to flow.

> *I am usually a person of many words, but I have no words to express the depth of my thanks for the beautiful book you sent me. I*

have just finished reading Tear Soup. *I cannot tell you how deeply it touched me.*

One of my daughter's and my favorite things to do was to cook. We both loved soup. . . .

I thought I could handle the pain. I am tough. I have handled a lot of pain, but this was different; it burned all the way to the bottom of my heart. I read stuff all the time that has made me believe that I shouldn't grieve. I should just be thankful that I was able to have that last conversation with Dee. I am thankful, but I miss her. I am thankful, but the pain keeps sideswiping me.

Today was such a dark day until I opened the book you took the time to send me. As I read the simple story, the dam broke and the tears that never have time to fall fell and fell and fell. I wept for what was and I wept for what is and I wept for my daughter, who I will miss every day of my life. Most of all I wept because you gave me permission to grieve and be angry and feel bitter without guilt.

I want you to know that I am going to continue to make my own recipe for "Tear Soup." I will stir up the grief, bitterness, anger, and loneliness and add to it the beauty of God's grace. . . .

May God bless and richly repay you for your kindness to me. I have hope now and I know the Father impressed you to send me this book. It was His way of telling me I will be okay and will survive this terrible thing.

All I can think as I read and weep, read and weep: *I was so sure that she needed anyone* **but** *me. I know nothing about loss. I am the last person on the face of this earth who should have been talking to a woman in the throes of unimaginable grief.*

I pause to wipe my eyes. *This was a need with my name on it. God sent me because . . .* I smile through tears as I realize the truth.

God sent me because she needed **me.**

As you take continual refuge in God, you'll see specific needs that clearly have your name on them. Recognizing these needs is a sacred expression of your unique God-given identity. Embrace them as opportunities in which the Holy Spirit leads you to be the hands and feet of Jesus in ways that nobody else can.

This is what happens when you do the hard work to lose who you're not and love who you are.

This is what it means to live your one life well.

now breathe

Start a list of needs with your name on them. Rephrase each one as an identity. For example, "I am a book-bestower." For inspiration, check out the list at ExhaleBook.com.

LIVE YOUR ONE LIFE WELL:

Live free to meet the need with your name on it.

eighteen

Live in Celebration:
You're Made to Seize the Yay!

Amy

I just didn't know. I never understood how much my parents loved me and longed for connection with me until I stood in their shoes. Until my boys became men and launched lives of their own.

I was the college freshman who skipped into the dorm, throwing a wave over my shoulder, not looking back. I was the fiercely independent girl who never lived at home again after that first departure. Instead, I looked for summer adventures and followed the opportunities into sublets and mission trips.

My parents and I were close, so I kept in touch. I didn't know what it felt like to wait for the phone calls . . . until now.

Now when my phone lights up with one of my sons' names, I light up like a Christmas tree. It's like my heart has been on hold until just that moment when it leaps from idle to overdrive. In my head, one profound word always pops up first: "Yay!!!"

Now I understand how my parents felt, because I feel it, too. This is what life is about. It's what our lives are for. We love people. We invest in them. We pray over them. And our story that's connected to theirs grows into part of the joy we experience in this life.

When asked what the greatest commandments are, Jesus laid out our call simply. Love God. Love others. That's it, but it's everything. Remember when the phrase *Carpe diem*, "Seize the day," became popularized? For Cheri and me, the core of this book is to stand on a desk and shout, "Seize the yay!" What's the "yay"? It's the love, the connections, the investments, and the *people*. Most of all the people.

A Time to Stop Talking

In our final dive into Scripture together, I want to look at Jesus's last interaction with His disciples, a chapter some call the High Priestly Prayer or "the *other* Lord's prayer." In this passage, He models what's important and shares the secrets of the life for which we long. He shows us clearly how to live our one life well.

At the finish of John 16, Jesus ends a discussion with His disciples and begins a conversation with His Father right in front of them. After a short introduction, the rest of chapter 17 is words in red, Jesus's words to His Father. This prayer is rich and deep. I can't begin to do it justice in one short chapter, but I want to touch on some points that put an endcap on our journey to exhale.

John starts the chapter with a transition. Jesus has been instructing His disciples about His looming arrest, but suddenly, He changes His focus and His audience. John says, "After Jesus said this, he looked toward heaven and prayed" (v. 1).

This may seem like a strange place to stop a moment, but it's crucial. I'm a girl who dearly loves to talk and process with her people, but there's a time to stop the discussion and pray. There's a moment when we have to turn our eyes to God and surrender.

Here at the end of this book is that time. We've worked through teaching and stories and ideas and exercises. We've lost who we're not. We've learned to love who we are. To really live our one life well, we have to turn to the Giver of Life. Our discussion draws to a close, and we focus our hearts on the One we love, praying that He would seal the lessons in us.

God, I need you in order to be able to change my life and exhale.

I want to lose who I'm not, eliminating forever hopelessness in the face of change, fear of failure, old labels, boundarylessness, rescuing, and floundering in sin.

I want to love who I am, embracing my uniqueness, my story, my personality, my quirks, my gifts, my calling, and my great need to be found by you. I rejoice in each of these gifts, created and given by you alone.

Finally, I want to live my one life well. I want to be a seed sender, fully alive and sharing your life. I desire to live the dreams you've planted in my heart and to move through this world restored. I want to seize the yay, lovingly holding my community, but I'm unable without your guidance and power. You're the only One who gives me the ability to change. Help me.

Jesus's first words to His Father were these:

Father, the hour has come. Glorify your Son, that your Son may glorify you. For you granted him authority over all people that he might give eternal life to all those you have given him.

vv. 1–2

When I was a little girl growing up in a traditional church, somehow I got the mistaken notion that it's selfish to pray for myself. Here Jesus sets an example, exploding my preconceptions. Jesus was *not* too insignificant to pray for himself, and neither are we. He prays for himself first while pointing every word to God's glory as the prayer's answer.

Like Jesus, we should pray for ourselves, and our ultimate answer to our prayers is that our lives glorify God. We can fix our heart on the end goal and ask.

Lord, I love you, and I only desire one thing. Use my life to bring you glory.

Then Jesus pulls the veil off of the meaning of life, saying it so clearly that there can be no question: "Now this is eternal life: that they know you, the only true God, and Jesus Christ, whom you have sent" (v. 3).

Knowing God is our life. Knowing Him is the very beginning to living our one life well. It's eternal life starting right now, not someplace down the road. It's not "out there" in heaven after we die. It's "in here" living life in God. As Acts 17:28 says, "For in him we live and move and have our being." Right now we can start living the eternal life that He gives to those who ask Him for it.

Lord, in the past, I've chosen the details of my life over eternal life. I lose those interruptions now and ask for the deepest pleasure given to humankind instead: knowing you. Today, I change my choice. Knowing you and following you are my focus. Let every other distraction that ruled me fall away.

Wrapping up the prayer for himself, Jesus praises God by saying, "I have brought you glory on earth by finishing the work you gave me to do" (John 17:4).

I have to confess that my heart skipped a beat when I read this. Recently, an old friend died. He had walked away from his relationship with Jesus decades ago, and the finality of his death sobered me. I thought about what I'll say to Jesus when I meet Him face-to-face. Even though my friend knew Jesus, he lived the majority of his life apart from Him. What could he say when he stood before Him with only a wasted life held in his hands? Surely he cried a flood of tears before he stepped into the place where we'll shed tears no more.

I don't know or understand a lot of things about that situation, but there's one thing I do know. I don't want that to be me. Or you. My heart's cry is that Jesus will say to us, "Well done, good and faithful servant" (Matthew 25:21), and our humble and honest reply will be, "I have brought you glory on earth by finishing the work you gave me to do."

Once we know the work that God has given us to do, and we're moving toward completing it, we can stand in full confidence both now and on that day in heaven, knowing that we're bringing God glory. It's the baseline definition of living our one life well, and an incomparable joy!

> *Lord, I want to stand before you at the end of my life knowing that I've used my gifts and fulfilled the calling you gave me. I need your direction to know what it is, and I need your power to do it. I look forward to the day when I can celebrate in your presence my fruitful seed-sender life and the way it's brought you glory!*

Knowing God and bringing Him glory is the essential first step toward our celebration, seizing the yay, but step two is loving people. Jesus, our ultimate mentor, didn't just tell others the two greatest commandments. Instead, every part of His life, magnified here at the end, displayed these truths.

They're Not All Mine

In the final sections of Jesus's prayer, He prays for His disciples, and then in a breathtaking move for His girls today, He prays for all who will believe in Him in the future.

Loving God. Loving people. That's the recipe for a life that counts. Taking those two steps creates a seize-the-yay life!

Every Sunday morning, I sit around a conference room table with a small band of women. We're a motley crew from every stage of life, and there's a lot of pain in that room. A lot of pain.

Behind every beautiful face, there's a story. There are stories of divorce and the saga of a missing husband. There are stories of chronic fatigue and chronicles of mental illness. There are tales of children lost to addiction and the helplessness of being a shut-in.

But most of all there are stories of God. How He's shown up and shown off. Of His faithfulness and compassion. Of His presence in the dark places and joy in the triumphs. The pain is real in our little room, but God is bigger.

There's no place I'd rather be on Sunday mornings than surrounded by women I love. It's a place of belonging, acceptance, and lots and lots of grace. They're my people, and I'm theirs. It's one of the places I'm called to live my one life well.

My overdeveloped sense of responsibility sometimes tells me that I owe everyone I meet the same kind of time and attention that I'm called to give my friends in our group. Jesus tells us something different. Here's how He prays:

> I have revealed you to those whom you gave me out of the world. They were yours; you gave them to me and they have obeyed your word. . . . I pray for them. I am not praying for the world, but for those you have given me, for they are yours.
>
> John 17:6, 9

But Some of Them Are Mine

Jesus has authority over all people (v. 2), loves the whole world, and came to die for everyone (John 3:16), but He recognized that these twelve men were uniquely His, given to Him by the Father. These are the ones He both loves and prays for.

Jesus found the ones who were His by listening to His Father. As He walked along, He tilted one ear toward The Voice and called the men given to Him. I'm learning to follow His example by praying, listening, and "calling," like in the formation of my class at church.

The women in my class are some of the people my Father has given to me. A handful of my neighbors are my assignment. I have friends and family that I know God has gifted me to care for. But you and I have limited time and energy, so it's important to know that in loving all, we're only *given* some. Whom have you been given? These people are your community.

When I processed these ideas with my husband, Barry, he pointed out a fact about plants that applies to us. Plants need other plants because that's how they're pollinated. There are no seeds without pollination.

In Jesus's prayer for His disciples, He stated that He had faithfully pointed them to God. What a picture. As we point to God, we pollinate. Pollination causes seeds to grow, and then the seeds are sent out. Jesus illustrates this exact picture when He says, "As you sent me into the world, I have sent them into the world" (John 17:18). Jesus, the Seed Grower, creates seed senders.

We each have other secondary callings, but for all of us who belong to the Father, we have two common primary callings. Just like Jesus modeled, we're called to know our Father and to point to Him.

Friend to friend. Mother to child. Neighbor to neighbor. This is how God's kingdom grows. What if we all followed Jesus's example, investing wholeheartedly in the people He's given us instead of being distracted by the crowds (hello, social media)? Our collection of real-life friends and family is community, and community is one of the big "yays" of life! A pollinating community is required for seed senders living their one life well.

Lord, I want to care well for those you've given me. Help me to put every distraction aside. Silence the noise of the crowd so that I can hear those who are mine. Show me who you've given to me, and I'll follow you to prioritize these people.

Love and Unity for All

Let these words from Jesus's prayer wash over you:

"Holy Father, protect them by the power of your name, the name you gave me, so that they may be one as we are one" (v. 11).

"I pray also for those who will believe in me through their message, that all of them may be one, Father, just as you are in me and I am in you" (vv. 20–21).

"I in them and you in me—so that they may be brought to complete unity. Then the world will know that you sent me and have loved them even as you have loved me" (v. 23).

> "I have made you known to them, and will continue to make you known in order that the love you have for me may be in them and that I myself may be in them" (v. 26).

In His prayer, Jesus reveals the threads that are woven into the fabric of His heart—love, oneness, and unity. I revel in that truth . . . and I *wrestle* with it.

In my fantasies, Jesus's priorities feed my hippy-fied heart. Love and peace, man! But in reality, I have a hard time living out these ideals. Just yesterday, halfway through writing this chapter, I received not one but two nasty-grams from a woman via social media. When I ignored the first one early in the day, trying to decide the best way to respond, the same disgruntled woman sent another with escalated emotion and condemnation. Bam! All my desire for love and unity went out the window in a split second.

But as I reflected, I realize that understanding John 17 should have helped my reactions. That woman on Facebook isn't one of the people that God has given to me. I don't have to waste time going back and forth explaining to her or trying to make her see things my way. Even though we know each other's names, we're strangers. We can agree to disagree, and I can exhale as I disconnect. On the other hand, I am called to show the world who Jesus is by the way I love her and the steps I take toward unity with her. Complicated stuff.

It's so beyond our natural selves, so we ask Christ for the things that He asked for us. We appeal to God for love and unity that overcome our horrible human reactions. When we send seeds of love into the soil of unity, fruit springs up! The woman who wants to exhale has to let go of the world's demands and simply follow Christ. Following Him means walking in love and cultivating unity.

Lord, we hold our community close, but we also want to move through the crowds with love and unity, showing your heart to the world.

Change for the End Game

Cheri and I believe that women have bought into a very destructive lie. In fact, for a period of our lives, we took out our little change purses and bought it, too.

Here's how the lie goes: I can fulfill the longings of my heart, meet the needs of the people in my life, or glorify God. I might be able to do a combination of two of these three things, but it's impossible to do all three. Jesus shows us how to battle this lie with His life.

Here's how He fulfilled the trifecta we want to achieve:

- **Glorifying God:** By living the Principle of Intention, saying only what the Father told Him to say and doing only what the Father told Him to do all the way to the cross, Jesus glorified God with His life. We'll do it imperfectly, but we can let listening to God transform us so that our words and actions glorify God, losing anything that's meant to go unspoken or undone.

- **Fulfilling the longings of our hearts:** Revealing His Father was the highest longing of Jesus's heart and the pinnacle of His mission. He did it by letting God shine through Him. Because we're made in God's image, filled with the gifts He's given us, we can tune our hearts to Jesus's wavelength. When our greatest desire is to reveal our Father through every part of our life, loving who He created us to be, we've started down a road to a seize-the-yay life.

- **Meeting the needs of our people:** Jesus was a people magnet who connected deeply wherever He went. He loved them all, but He claimed a small group as His own. In following God's voice, He met all their true needs. Our people will get our best when we stop following the cries of the crowd to focus on the still, small voice. Living your one life well benefits your people.

As we finish this book, lay it down, and turn back to our everyday world, there are two temptations that we'll all face: conformity and withdrawal. Conformity will cause us to forget the lessons we've learned. Instead of seeking God for strength each day to lose who we're not, we'll gradually begin to give up and give in to external forces like unrealistic expectations simply because it's easier in the moment. Withdrawing is another form of seeking temporary ease. Being alone instead of in a tight-knit community seems less costly. After all, the cat doesn't talk back (much). But isolation keeps us from living our one life well. Pollination, remember?

Jesus neither conformed nor withdrew. At all cost, He defied the world's standards to glorify His Father. He created community with love and unity despite the mess He had to wade through to do it.

When we live our priorities, cultivating the fruit of our lives, we'll reap these benefits:

- the joy of investing the gifts God has given us
- the peace of serving others within God's will
- the soul-satisfaction of bringing God glory through love and unity

Cheri and I aren't foolish enough to promise you that you won't be busy or that you won't sometimes lay awake at 2:37 a.m. We want for you what we're experiencing little by little for ourselves. Powered by God and surrendered to change, we can move from the pain of running on empty to enjoying happy tired.

From here, Lord, we launch out in faith, believing that our desires, our people's needs, and God's glory aren't mutually exclusive. We want to live in the fullness of your life. Empower us to change. Cause us to pause to listen to you before we utter yes. Make us committed to unearth your gifts and invest them. Help us to exhale and to bring your breath of life into every room. Give us the compelling desire to live for your glory. Amen.

❊ now breathe

Before you close this book, leaf through the pages of this chapter, taking a few minutes to read the italicized prayers out loud. Sit for a time in silence to hear God's words to you.

LIVE YOUR ONE LIFE WELL:

Live in celebration of God's fullest life in you.

Part Three Quick Reference Guide to
Live Your ONE Life Well

Live as a vibrant seed sender.
Live open to God's direction and redirection.
Live free to meet the need with your name on it.
Live in celebration of God's fullest life in you.

Old Mindset . . .	*New Mindset* . . .
My job is to slog through the next thing in front of me.	God made me to be a seed sender who grows His kingdom.
I must make my ultimate dream come true.	I follow God's lead as each dream seeds the next.
I have to work hard to transform myself.	Jesus invites me to take refuge in Him and become fully restored by Him.
I'm stuck in the life I have.	The Spirit empowers me for my fullest life in Christ when I turn to Him.

Conclusion

You may be at the end of the book, but this doesn't have to be good-bye. In fact, we hope it's just the beginning of our journey together.

We would love to hear from you! Share your success stories: how you're losing who you're NOT, loving who you ARE, and living your ONE life well. You can drop us an email at AmyNCheri@GritNGraceGirls.com.

Check out the practical printable *Exhale* resources we've created for you at ExhaleBook.com/resources. Look especially for the quarterly reassessment so you can track your progress.

Exhale with friends! You'll find small-group materials, including a reader's study guide and leader's discussion guide ready for you to download at ExhaleBook.com/study.

We'd like to close with a prayer for you:

We kneel before the Father,

from whom every family in heaven and on earth derives its name.

We pray that out of His glorious riches He may strengthen you

with power through His Spirit in your inner being,

so that Christ may dwell in your hearts through faith.

And we pray that you, being rooted and established in love,

may have power, together with all the Lord's holy people,

to grasp how wide and long and high and deep is the love of Christ,

and to know this love that surpasses knowledge—

that you may be filled to the measure of all the fullness of God.

Now to Him who is able to do immeasurably more
than all we ask or imagine,

according to His power that is at work within us,

to Him be glory in the church and in Christ Jesus
throughout all generations,

for ever and ever!

Amen.

Ephesians 3:15–21 (paraphrased)

Love Who You ARE
Personality Quiz

Instructions: For each scenario, circle the one response that is most true for you. If two are equally true, circle them both.

1. *I wear clothes that . . .*

   C are flashy, fun, and sometimes elicit compliments from complete strangers.

   I are understated, classic, and often monochromatic.

   D make a statement and serve multiple purposes with minimum fuss.

   R are comfortable. Really comfortable.

2. *At a large social gathering full of people I've never met, I'm likely to*

   C have a wonderful time working the room . . . in an hour or two, I'll be in the center telling stories and making everyone laugh.

   I I seek out one person with whom I can have a meaningful quiet conversation.

D find a way to be useful.

R sit and entertain myself, perhaps by people-watching.

3. **When there's a conflict between me and someone I care about, the worst thing they can do is**

C quit talking to me; give me the cold shoulder.

I make inaccurate assumptions about my motives.

D waste my time with drawn-out discussions and needless drama.

R raise their voice.

4. **Complete this sentence: "I do things . . .**

C the fun way!"

I the right way."

D MY way."

R the least stressful way."

5. **If we're planning a trip together, you'll be smart to ask me to . . .**

C take tons of selfies and "us-ies" and post them to Instagram so all our friends can join us virtually.

I plan our itinerary and packing lists.

D deal with unexpected challenges (i.e., getting us food vouchers if our flight is delayed . . . telling pushy hucksters to back off . . .).

R show up an hour earlier than you actually need me to be at the airport.

6. **My home/desk/purse/car organization method is best described:**

C It's all in here somewhere!

I A place for everything, and everything in its place.

D I only keep what I use.

R I'm not using it now . . . but I might need it some day.

7. *When coaching or mentoring, taking a(n) _____ approach feels most natural for me.*

   C   collaborative leadership

   I   servant leadership

   D   transformational leadership

   R   authentic leadership

8. *I have the hardest time resting when . . .*

   C   I know someone is upset with me. I can't sleep until we've talked it out and made things right.

   I   there's a mistake in a project I'm working on. I will stay up late fixing it until it's fixed; only then can I relax enough to fall asleep.

   D   I haven't finished my to-do list. It's worth staying up late to get it all done and then get some "power sleep."

   R   others around me are upset or hurting. Once I've helped them through their problems, I can rest easy.

9. *I tend to be a _____ learner.*

   C   verbal

   I   visual

   D   auditory

   R   hands-on

10. *My elementary school report cards had comments like*

   C   "_____ is such a delight—always ready with a smile. She does struggle to keep track of her personal belongings, and she needs to remember to raise her hand before speaking up in class."

   I   "_____ is a conscientious student who has unbroken rows of gold stars for turning in all of her work on time. She needs to accept that an A- is still an A . . . not an F."

D "_____ is a natural leader. She often takes charge of organizing the games at recess. In the classroom, she needs to learn how to follow directions, take turns, and avoid back-talk."

R "_____ is always the first to ask, 'Mrs. _____, how can I help you today?' and to lend a helping hand to other students. She needs to learn to ask for help as well as offer it."

11. *When it comes to receiving public recognition . . .*

C I'll buy a new dress and have my hair done; I love the attention, the chance to make a speech, and the photo op!

I it's mortifying, especially when I find myself unexpectedly in the spotlight. Write me a note or send me a text . . . please?

D I want it to focus on *why* what I did made a difference for people. Spare me any meaningless fanfare.

R how about you give me a Starbucks gift card instead? And then we can skip the ceremony and hang out together.

12. *If I were put on bed rest for a month, I would need*

C lots of people to visit me to keep me from getting lonely.

I a second opinion and plenty of my own research to make sure that bed rest really was the right choice.

D my laptop and high-speed internet so I could stay on top of my work.

R the remote control and maybe a good book or two.

13. *When I don't have _____ in my life, I quickly become unpleasant to be around.*

C enjoyment

I order

D achievement

R peace

14. *My method of packing for a trip involves . . .*

    C discovering that I have nothing fit to wear. So I rush out for a last-minute shopping spree to get fun new clothes, shoes, and accessories.

    I opening the "My Packing List" file on my computer, printing it out, and following it. At least two days prior to leaving; a week if possible.

    D pulling out my carry-on and packing the bare minimum; preferably mix-and-match and easily hand-washables.

    R not sweating it. I can always buy anything I forget once I arrive at my destination.

15. *When I make a mistake, it bothers me because . . .*

    C one little mistake can ruin all my plans for having a great day.

    I I'm a perfectionist; I live in constant "error terror."

    D I hate anything that slows down my progress toward a goal.

    R other people sometimes have such strong reactions to my mistakes.

16. *Which of these thoughts is most likely to be keeping you awake at 2:37 a.m.?*

    C *I can't believe they didn't laugh at any of my funny stories. I told all my best ones! Why didn't they like me?*

    I *I can't believe she didn't call or text to wish me a happy birthday. If she really cared, she would have remembered.*

    D *I can't believe I had to waste time in a long boring meeting. It's time for a little less talk and a lot more action.*

    R *I can't believe the way people interrupt each other and shout each other down these days. It's so disrespectful.*

17. *Imagine that a new community theater opens up in your town. Which of these roles are you most drawn to?*

    C the star, performing front and center

    I the producer, working behind the scenes to get all the details right

    D the director, telling everyone exactly what to do and how

    R an audience member, happily sitting back and enjoying the show

18. *If you were to audio record yourself for a day and listen to the replay, you'd expect to hear . . .*

    C loud exclamations of "Yes!" and "Wow!" and plenty of laughter.

    I sounds of concern, like "uh-oh" and "nuh-uh" and "tsk-tsk."

    D directive words, like "Now . . ." and "Next . . ." and "I want you to . . ."

    R neutral affirmatives, like "Oh" and "I see" and "I hear you."

19. *Some criticisms you've heard through the years—to your face or behind your back—include (or are similar to) . . .*

    C "motor mouth" . . . "Pollyanna" . . . "attention-seeker."

    I "know-it-all" . . . "impossible to please" . . . "rigid" . . . "downer."

    D "bossy pants" . . . "emasculating" . . . "unfeminine."

    R "lazy bones" . . . "wishy-washy" . . . "moocher."

20. *When a friend is going through a crisis, your natural reaction is to . . .*

    C offer encouragement and hope.

    I point her to the best resources.

D take care of immediate physical needs (meals, child care, laundry, etc.).

R be present for her.

21. **Which quote resonates most with you?**

C "Laughter is the shortest distance between two people."

I "The difference between something good and something great is attention to detail."

D "Winning isn't everything, but it beats anything that comes in second."

R "Peace is its own reward."

22. **Which Scripture is the best match for you?**

C "Rejoice in the Lord always. I will say it again: Rejoice!" Philippians 4:4

I "May he give you the desire of your heart and make all your plans succeed." Psalm 20:4

D "Dear children, let us not love with words or speech but with actions and in truth." 1 John 3:18

R "Let the peace of Christ rule in your hearts, since as members of one body you were called to peace." Colossians 3:15

23. **Which of these thoughts is most likely to be running through your head?**

C *I just can't wait! Next weekend is going to be such a blast! Counting down the days!*

I *I'll follow the recipe word-for-word since this is my first time trying it.*

D *If I just shuffle my schedule around a bit . . . like this . . . I can easily squeeze in a new project!*

R *Pizza isn't my thing, but this is what everyone else wanted. It's all good. No biggie.*

24. *What do you dislike most about text messaging?*

   C You wish there were more emojis so you could really express yourself.

   I You have to fix all the mistakes made by autocorrect.

   D You'd rather leave a voice message—it's faster.

   R You'd rather talk in person—it's less effort.

25. *What kind of gift would you most enjoy receiving?*

   C a shared social experience, like a movie or play or concert or dinner out

   I something that shows that the giver knows my personal preferences

   D a gift certificate so I can choose what I really want

   R something with no strings attached—it irks me when "gifts" are obligations in disguise

Now, add up your totals:

   C Connector = _____

   I Inspector = _____

   D Director = _____

   R Reflector = _____

Your highest score correlates with your primary personality type, and your next highest score indicates your secondary personality type.

Glossary

animated—to be brought fully and vibrantly to life

calling—first drawing close to Jesus and then going, being sent out in His Spirit to do His work

competent mistakes—normal, natural "oops" moments that occur during any trial-and-error learning process throughout our lives; not to be confused with intentional wrong choices, moral failures, or sins

defining moment—a past event that influences, and even controls, current choices without our knowledge, permission, or intention; not to be confused with intentionally holding a grudge or refusing to forgive

dis-appointing—intentionally rescinding authority from any person who has taken too much authority or been given too much authority; not to be confused with failing to honor commitments or breaking promises or being irresponsible

faux-pology—a knee-jerk apology given when none is necessary or when "I'm sorry" doesn't even make sense, such as apologizing to the wall you just bumped into; a habitual appeasement strategy common with people-pleasers

fixed mindset—a thought process that sees all our abilities and talents as preset and unalterable. People with a fixed mindset think that you're either "good at it" or not. There's no room in this mindset for growth or change.

growth mindset—a thought process that sees all our abilities and talents in terms of a process, continually growing through learning and even mistakes; this mindset sees every start as a seed and everything after the start as a growth opportunity

pray-cess—to process a problem or concern via reflective, conversational, ongoing prayer

preemptive flip—when we heed God's warnings in His Word and through His Spirit about our weaknesses so that we can tap into His strength, thereby avoiding a looming failure, sin, or consequence

Principle of Intention—Jesus lived by the Principle of Intention, saying only what the Father told Him to say and doing only what the Father told Him to do; we can follow His pattern and improve our lives by doing what He did, listening to our Father and then doing and saying *only* what He tells us to do and say (John 8:28)

problem preventer—someone who tries to preempt problems from occurring by anticipating what could go wrong and stopping it before it begins; problem-preventing becomes meddling when it's not requested, not needed, or stunts the necessary maturity that comes from experiencing normal pain and disappointment; a parent who is a problem-preventer may be called a "snowplow parent" or "lawnmower parent"

redemptive flip—we can reach to Jesus for redemption after a failure, sin, or consequence through repentance. Praise the Redeemer!

quirk—a unique trait hardwired by God that may make you an outsider

seed sender—a person who shares her God-given gifts and His love with the world in a people-transforming and kingdom-building way

setting a boundary—choosing God's direction over someone's expectation

square breathing—a method of inhaling, holding, and exhaling in counts of four that prevents hyperventilation and calms the symptoms of anxiety

Acknowledgments

Amy's

Writing my first book, *Breaking Up with Perfect*, was a painful process—so painful that I swore I would *never* do it again. The writing was hard. The isolation was excruciating, and the process was brutal. Anyway . . . what's the saying? "We plan and God laughs." Yes, He must have laughed, but He's never left me alone. In fact, God's given me himself and His people in delightful abundance.

God, I thank you first. Your ways are higher than my ways, and your thoughts are higher than mine, too. I planned never to write another book, but you patiently drew me until I was willing to follow you, even there. Thank you for your presence, your Word, and the messages you've placed like a burning coal in my heart. Thank you most of all for a co-author!

Cheri Gregory, you are a treasure. You reached out to me in the pit I was in after book #1 and created a partnership that has fed my soul the last three years. I love processing life with you through many, many words.

Barry, through every high and every single low, you've been there encouraging, spurring on, and smoking meat for dinner. You're my favorite person on the planet, and I love that you make me laugh every day. You're a rock, and you totally rock.

Anson and Nolan, being your mom has made me a better person. As I've watched you grow into men, I'm so proud of the people you've become. (And now that you're adults, I'm exhaling a little bit!)

Although Facebook friends are fun, there's nothing like the women who are in your everyday life. For those who have walked and talked . . . chatted with toes in the sand . . . celebrated birthdays . . . met in downtown Raleigh for lunch . . . sat around a conference table . . . shared and cried and prayed . . . you know who you are, and you're a lifeline for me. I love you beyond measure.

Kathi Lipp, there's no one like you. Your encouragement, your belief in me, and the doors of opportunity that you've held open have been transforming. I'm forever grateful.

The Proverbs 31 Ministries team, you've walked with me from the beginning of my ministry journey, and I'm thankful that I've never had to do it without you.

This book wouldn't be nearly the same without our Manuscript Development Team. Your countless hours of reading our original mess—I mean drafts—and your insightful critique have benefited every reader of this book. We couldn't have done it without you. Thank you, thank you!

A special shout-out to my favorite member of the Manuscript Development Team, Megan Dohm. Usually it's not nice to have favorites, but since Megan is my niece, it's allowed. You are gifted and wise beyond your years. Thank you for walking through two books with me. I can't wait until the day that I'm on your Manuscript Development Team.

To all the women we've interviewed for *Grit 'n' Grace*, thank you, thank you for letting Cheri and me be part of the conversation.

Blythe Daniel, you are invaluable. I hear about lots of literary agents, but none hold a candle to you as far as caring so much and so well. You've gently walked this reluctant writer through the process once again. You deserve a medal.

Kim Bangs and Bethany House, from the first minute of our first meeting, we chose you (and then prayed for a contract!). We had a feeling this was going to be a great ride, and it has been. Your wise editing, planning, and communication have made this a stellar process. I can't believe that I'm so happy at the end of writing a second book, but I am. What a revelation!

Cheri's

Amy Carroll, my candid cheerleader and gentle challenger, I love your willingness to listen to my latest idea and let me throw you under the bus in the outtakes. It tickles me positively pink that you actually enjoyed writing this book. I am grateful to Skype and Southwest for helping us do life and ministry together from opposite coasts!

Kathi Lipp, for being the safest person in my life. Because of you, I've risked more, failed more, learned more, and had more fun than I ever dreamed. You're also the most generous person I know; you've made possible so much of what I love doing these days. Thanks for letting me be the *woe* to your *woo*, the *oww* to your *wow*.

Michele Cushatt, for being a comforting friend who both eases my pain and strengthens my core. Thank you for making me feel seen, heard, and understood . . . and applying a well-timed boot to my backside.

Emily Freeman, for getting through my thick skull that I can impress my critics *or* serve my audience. And the amazing women of The Artist's Bench—Angela, Anjuli, Erin, Marian, Melissa, Meredith, Kamille, and Shaina—y'all handed me virtual Kleenexes when my book proposal was rejected and waved emoji pom-poms when I declared, "I'm starting a podcast." I'm so grateful for all I learned from each one of you during our Voxer conversations.

Our FABULOUS team of *Grit 'n' Grace* interns: Shantell Brightman, Kendra Burrows, Amanda Davison, Kimberli Freilinger, Kate Hollimon, Kelsee Keitel, and Tammy Littlejohn—the first daring seven who jumped on board even though we warned you that we had no clue what we were doing!—Iris Bryant, Jenn Bryant, Leigh Ellen Eades, Sarah Geringer, Shannon Geurin, Liana George, Jeanette Hanscome, Tonya Kubo, Rachel Latham, Jamia Lewis, Melissa McLamb, Kristin Milner, Chris Moss, Denise Pass, Vicki Stone, and Lori Young. Thank you for all your prayers, enthusiasm, support, and hard work that make the podcast possible each week. It's an honor to be a part of your ministries and to see how God continues to lead you!

Tonya Kubo, for leading the *Grit 'n' Grace* Facebook page and group. And for being a great sounding board and brainstorming buddy; I love coach-aborating with you!

Shantell Brightman, I'm so grateful God knew I needed you in my life! I don't know what I'd do without your friendship, your support, your processes, and your skill at herding my squirrels.

The *Exhale* Manuscript Development Team, who kept us motivated and encouraged and prayed up. The hours you poured into our early drafts made this such a better book!

Kendra Burrows, for leading the *Exhale* Manuscript Development Team, being my long-lost twin, and ministering to me in such a myriad of ways. I can't wait to be on your MDT one day!

Kim Bangs, for the last year, I've giddily shoehorned "our editor, Kim Bangs" into every conceivable conversation. Thank you for championing this message and guiding us through its refinement.

Steve Laube, I tell everyone that I have The Best Agent Ever. Thank you for staunchly believing in me during the rejection years. And for coming up with such amazing titles!

Annemarie and Jonathon, I'm so glad you picked me to be your mom.

Daniel, you've seen the good, the bad, and the ugly for thirty-three years, and you still believe in me, support me, and love me. You're my favoritest husband!

Jesus, thank you for rescuing me, delighting in me, and inviting me to take refuge in you alone.

Do you want your Exhale journey
to have greater impact?

Gather a group of friends to go through the study.

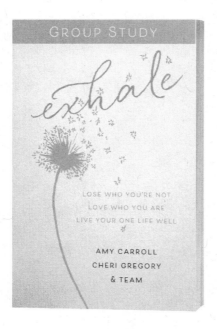

Work together to lose who you're not,
love who you are, and live your one life well.

ExhaleBook.com/Study

Grit 'n' Grace

>>>>— GOOD GIRLS BREAKING BAD RULES ——→

Our partnership was birthed through the *Grit 'n' Grace* podcast, and we'd love for you to continue to connect with us there! The podcast is for you if

- you're a "good girl" who loves Jesus
- you long to experience the abundant life He's promised
- some days, you feel like a puppet, with perfectionism and people-pleasing pulling all your strings

We believe every good girl can grow her grit, embrace God's grace, and learn to break bad rules.

Pull up a seat at the table and listen to *Grit 'n' Grace* each week by subscribing at gritngracegirls.com or through Apple Podcasts or Stitcher.

Proverbs 31
MINISTRIES

If you were inspired by this book and desire to deepen your own personal relationship with Jesus Christ, I encourage you to connect with Proverbs 31 Ministries.

Proverbs 31 Ministries exists to be a trusted friend who will take you by the hand and walk by your side, leading you one step closer to the heart of God through these resources:

- Free online daily devotions
- First 5 Bible study app
- Daily radio program
- Books and resources
- Online Bible studies
- COMPEL Training: www.CompelTraining.com

To learn more about Proverbs 31 Ministries, call 877-731-4663 or visit www.Proverbs31.org.

Proverbs 31 Ministries

630 Team Rd., Suite 100

Matthews, NC 28105

www.Proverbs31.org

Amy Carroll loves connecting a community through cultivating tender hearts and strong voices. There's nothing that delights her heart more than moving through life with Jesus and her tribe of tender-spoken women.

Amy is the author of *Breaking Up with Perfect*, a member of the Proverbs 31 Ministries speaker and writer teams, and co-host of the *Grit 'n' Grace* podcast. She loves traveling all over the world and adores hearing the God-stories of women at her events.

As a consummate southern girl, Amy loves words that shape a great story and a challenging idea. She writes monthly devotions for *Encouragement for Today* and weekly blog posts at amycarroll.org, and revels in podcast conversations with Cheri Gregory at gritngracegirls.com. She has been interviewed on numerous podcasts as well as radio programs, including *Focus on the Family*.

Amy also loves to help other speakers give birth to their messages. She is the founder and speaker coach of Next Step Coaching Services, which provides one-on-one training for Christian speakers and writers.

Wife, mom, daughter, and friend are Amy's favorite roles. You can find her in North Carolina on any given day texting her two adult sons, typing at her computer, hanging out with her hunky husband, or trying to figure out one more alternative to cooking dinner. Share life with Amy by connecting with her:

Her website and blog: amycarroll.org

Her speaker coaching services: nextstepcoachingservices.com

Facebook: @amydohmcarroll

Instagram: @amydohmcarroll

To inquire about having Amy speak for your next event, visit proverbs31.org/speakers or call the Proverbs 31 Ministries office at 1-877-731-4663.

Through Scripture and storytelling, **Cheri Gregory** loves sharing experiences that connect to women's frustrations, fears, and failures, giving them hope that they are not alone—someone gets them. She delights in helping women draw closer to Jesus: the strength of every tender heart.

As paradigm-shifter, Cheri believes that "how-to" works best in partnership with "heart, too." She loves engaging in conversations that lead to transformations via Skype interviews with Amy and *Grit 'n' Grace* podcast guests.

Cheri is the co-author, with Kathi Lipp, of *You Don't Have to Try So Hard* and *Overwhelmed*; the co-host of the *Grit 'n' Grace* podcast; and the co-leader of Sensitive and Strong: the place for the HSP woman to find community. She also serves as the curriculum director and alumni coordinator for Leverage: The Speaker Conference.

She is working on a PhD in leadership, researching the leadership journeys of influential Christian women bloggers. She has spent the last quarter of a century teaching junior high, high school, and college English, and currently teaches AP English literature and composition at a small Christian boarding school.

Cheri also loves to help speakers move their message from the stage to the page. Through Write Beside You, she offers one-on-one coaching and online eCourses for Christian speakers and writers.

Cheri has been "wife of my youth" to Daniel, her opposite personality, for thirty years. She is mom to two young adults, Annemarie and Jonathon, who are also opposite personalities. The Gregory family suffers for Jesus on the central California coast.

Her websites: CheriGregory.com and SensitiveAndStrong.com

Her writer coaching services: WriteBesideYou.com

Facebook: @Cheri.Gregory.Author

Instagram: @cheri_gregory

To inquire about having Cheri speak for your next event, visit her website at CheriGregory.com/contact or email Info@CheriGregory.com.